Table of Contents

Preface ix
Acknowledgments xiii
Introduction 1
Part One 7

Red Flag Terms 8

Persuasive Words 9

Stories and Metaphors	10	Emotional Words	21
Double-Bind	12	Pacing	23
Contingency	14	Questions	26
Rapport	14	Missing Words	29
Authority	19	Absolutes	30
Humor	20		

Fallacies 34

Loaded Questions	42	Personal Attack	49
Misrepresentation	44	Burden of Proof	50
After This, Because of This	46	Either- Or	52
Circular Reasoning	46	Generalization	53
Face Value	47	Ignoring the Issue	56
False Cause	48	Contradiction	57

Intent Signals 58

Us vs Them	62	Righteous Indignation	73
Supremacy	68	Intimidation	75
Absolute Certainty	71	Affiliations	76

Part Two 79

Rushing the Animals 80

Primary Species	81	High Protein Cows	97
Dominion	86	A Foolish Notion	99
Only a Moron	91	Head First	102
Twaddle	95		

Doing the Limbaugh 105

Dr. Waters	106	The Cuyahoga River	115
Pinatubo	111	The Best	117
Punishment	113		

Hanging in Limbaugh 121

The Biggest Threat	122	Almost Nothing	130
Hard Cases	124	Dogma Food	131
A Moral Imperative	128		

Fools Rush In 133

Little Expertise	134	Powerful Forces	140
Their Position is Absurd	135	Degree of Savagery	143
Hogwash	137	We Are Only Part of It	146

Conclusion 148
References Cited 153
Bibliography 157
Index 159
About the Author 165

PREFACE

Fame is proof that people are gullible.
                         --Ralph Waldo Emerson

Criticism is never very easy to accept, even when it is constructive. If we are not ready for it, or if the cost of changing our ways is too great, we try to ignore it. If it is too frank, we may become resentful and attempt to turn the tables back upon the critic. Either way, such responses are not often in our best interest.

Environmental backlash is the public's retort to years of criticism for doing, as Rush Limbaugh says, "what comes naturally." The reaction has been fueled by many emotions. Defensive egos, fear for loss of wealth or convenience, frustration with the enormity of the challenges, anger with misinformation, indignation in response to moral extremists, and avoidance of guilt all contribute. As with most rebellion against criticism, the results may not be good for us. Backlash is already causing reduced financial contributions to environmental organizations. People are beginning to ignore sound ecological research. These are the first steps toward stifling environmental progress.

Not knowing what to believe about environmental issues also makes us vulnerable to backlash rhetoric. One day we believe there is an ozone problem. The next day someone convinces us we were wrong. Our confusion comes from our frequent inability to be objective while listening to persuasive language. This is why most states have laws that give us three days to change our minds if someone sells us something we didn't want or couldn't afford. The laws recognize the power of the professional salesperson to persuade us. Unfortunately, there is no three-day opportunity for rescission when it comes to making decisions about the environment.

However, if we could recognize the validity of a particular argument immediately upon hearing it, a significant degree of objective analysis could occur during the "sales pitch." We could screen the words of the speaker and separate facts from figments. **The Bum's Rush** teaches this skill, for in the arena of environmental politics, "buyers remorse" could have dire consequences.

I have chosen Rush Limbaugh's statements about environmental issues because they typify the kind of persuasive language that can mislead us, and because they exemplify backlash parlance. Furthermore, with a listening audience of more than twenty million Americans a week, their influence is significant. Considering that many of his arguments are indeed misleading, as we will see, an investigation of his particular exhortations may be especially valuable.

To illustrate the persuasive words and the logical fallacies Limbaugh uses, I have selected phrases from his two books rather than from his broadcasts in most instances. I believe these provide for a more accurate appraisal of his remarks. Although most of his published statements were spoken to his radio and television audience, writing them down has given him the opportunity to be more careful with how he presents his arguments. Also, using quotes from his books gives the reader a chance to review sentences in their complete context, so as to confirm I have not misrepresented the intent of his argument.

I have not singled out Rush Limbaugh because I think he is "The Most Dangerous Man in America", as his opponents have dubbed him. To the contrary, every person who says frankly what he thinks is doing a public service. Limbaugh's prominence has the potential of making a healthy contribution to the environmental debate. The only requirement is that we apply the message of this book when listening to him or any other persuader. Illogic, fallacies, psycholinguistic strategies, and propaganda are intrinsic to the language of people besides Limbaugh who influence public opinion. Such individuals solicit people to choose sides as in a football arena, rather than encourage independent thinking and mutual cooperation. As P.J. O'Rourke says in **Parliament of**

Whores, "both Democrats and Republicans are guilty of mindless sports-fan behavior, rat-gagging gluttony for political office, and ideology without ideas." (O'Rourke, 1991, p.19)

Although I intend no personal attack on Rush Limbaugh, I do demonstrate that many of his statements are misleading. Samuel Johnson once said, "Every man has a right to utter what he thinks is truth, and every other man has a right to knock him down for it." I think it would be best to say, "every other man has the right to ask him to show his cards." Anyway, it is seldom the orator who ultimately creates dangerous conditions. It is the blind followers of his gospel. Mr. Limbaugh, like speakers on both sides of the environmental debate, says some things that may be accurate, and some things that may not be. It is up to us to learn which is which. This is difficult in an age when we cannot possibly research all of the vital issues as carefully as we might want. It is understandable how we become prejudiced to one way of thinking, or to one favored speaker.

Prejudice born of ignorance, however, is not always excusable, especially with matters of great consequence. Therefore, we should not act on the advice of a singular source, without weighing the evidence, investigating the references, and reflecting upon the conclusions they support. Such logical analysis does not lessen the value of faith. According to Samuel Butler, "You can do very little with faith, but you can do nothing without it." Faith, however, should be balanced with reason. It is upon this balance our future may depend.

Acknowledgments

As no man is an island, no book is the result of an author's labor alone. I am grateful to my father-in-law, Johann Samlowski, for sending me the broadcast of Rush Limbaugh that initially motivated my investigation of environmental backlash and persuasive fallacies. I also learned much from Johann's viewpoint, especially when it differed from mine. Of course, his daughter was his most valuable contribution. Her painstaking editing of the manuscript after a day of editing a newspaper, her willingness to confront my own reaction to criticism, and her continual love, support and good humor have been invaluable.

I also want to acknowledge the research efforts of my daughter, Jessica. Her enthusiasm for this work has been encouraging, in spite of the geographical distance that separates us. For his commitment and professionalism, I want to thank Patrick Eskridge for making the appearance of the text as perfect as its message is important. I thank Lorry Roberts, of Legendary Publishing, for a vision and courage not common to many other publishers. Finally, to the librarians at Boise State University who often found what I couldn't, the friends who tolerated my absence from shared recreation (including my horse, Brioso), and to the many authors of books on persuasion and environmentalism, whose ideas contribute to this book, I offer my sincere appreciation.

INTRODUCTION

*Words are the most potent drug
that mankind uses.*
                        --Rudyard Kipling

We live in an age when decisions made by the body politic can have far-reaching and possibly irreversible consequences. Some might argue that those who influence public opinion should be morally accountable for disaster resulting from their persuasive efforts. Such an assumption of responsibility is not likely, however. It is a better argument to place this burden on the public who responds to persuasion inappropriately. We should make every reasonable effort to verify the soundness of a persuader's words. Unfortunately, very few people are familiar enough with the strategies of persuasion to know when rhetoric is fallacious. Few colleges even list courses in persuasion. (Dietrich, 1976, p. 192)

So, think of **The Bum's Rush** as "Practical Persuasion 101." It is practical for three reasons. First, it focuses on the environment and on environmental backlash, two of the most important subjects in current affairs. Second, it discusses the specific oratory

1

of one of the most popular persuaders in America today, oratory that significantly contributes to the backlash phenomenon. Third, it embraces all three means of
persuasion, namely:

· the ability to stir the emotions of an audience
· the logical supports of a persuasive argument
· the character of the speaker

These three categories, set forth by Aristotle more
than twenty-five hundred years ago as pathos, logos
and ethos, create the structure of **Part One.**

The first category introduces language that can stir
our emotions, and even bypass critical thinking. It reveals persuasive words and phrases that trigger unconscious processes. These are powerful techniques of
communication used and misused for centuries by religious leaders, diplomats, ad designers, sales agents,
physicians, educators and lawyers.

Persuasive words play on the natural tendency our
brains have to respond automatically to certain kinds
of language. This becomes more profound when our
conscious attention is diminished, but the inclination
always exists, for every word we hear is processed at
both a conscious and an unconscious level. To take advantage of this, a speaker need do only four things:
He needs to use language that holds our attention. He
must present ideas that are difficult to disagree with.

He has to increase our readiness to respond to his ideas. And, he needs to provide us with specific suggestions to act upon.

In his famous book, **The Origin of Consciousness in the Breakdown of the Bicameral Mind,** Julian Jaynes presents a historical perspective on the influencing power of words. He attributes the earliest use of words to Gods, who spoke to man before he himself could speak. (Jaynes, 1966) (According to Jaynes, the gods spoke in poetry. This perhaps explains our adoration of singers and poets.) As man began speaking, words had the most hypnotic characteristics when a "collective unconscious" pervaded a society, and when spoken by a figure of authority. In our times, with worldwide information technology being what it is, such a collective unconscious can easily evolve. This can give power to any prominent public speaker who understands the collective viewpoint.

In spite of the potency of such words, it is important to realize that persuasive language cannot control us or our thoughts, unless we let it. It can, however, unduly influence us if we are caught off guard. With an awareness of the techniques of persuasion, we will learn to feel when "truth" does not follow the speaker's direction.

The second category of persuasive language describes logical and illogical fallacies. Although most of these have been studied since the time of Aristotle, very few people in modern times are knowledgeable about them, in spite of the fact they are used constantly in persuasion. Specific fallacies are named, defined, then illustrated with typical backlash comments.

The last category defines "red flags" that relate to the intentions of a speaker or writer, and explains how they can influence objectivity. These "intent signals" are revealed when people speak from a position of defensiveness, or when self-interests are more important than "truth." Sometimes the intention of the speaker shows he has been unwilling to consider another view point. Such a person may truly believe what he* is saying. Innocent intent signals are as likely to lead to fallacies as less ethical ones.

In **Part Two**, we examine statements Rush Limbaugh has made in his books and on his broadcasts regarding environmental issues. The numbers, corresponding to each red flag found in his rhetoric, are listed immediately after the entire statement. By using the numbers to refer to the list and/or its definitions, you can verify correct answers and test your ability to recognize and name the various communication techniques. Following the numerical references, words and phrases illustrating the strategies are discussed.

---

*For simplicity, male gender pronouns will be used throughout the text to refer to both male and female subjects. Note also that the use of "Limbaugh" in place of Mr. Limbaugh intends no disrespect. This will also expedite concise reading.

Truth, an essential concept in a study of persuasion, is admittedly amorphous. According to an old proverb, it is located at the bottom of a well. When we look for it, we see only our reflection. This says that each path is true for the person who is traversing it. We learn, and hopefully grow, from each path until our unique reality begins to resonate with a higher, more universal one. These philosophical ideas do have support in science. For example, the Heisenberg Principle, which says the act of observing can change what is being observed, is continually being demonstrated in many areas of research.

To bring our understanding of things into accord with this higher level of awareness is not an easy task. It requires letting go of our desperate hold on ideologies, egos and identities that represent our individual and collective assumptions. This happens automatically when we listen with open minds. **The Bum's Rush** offers tools that can be used to gain this comprehension, but the reader must make a conscious effort to use them. If after applying this material to the words a person is using to persuade you (or to reinforce what you already think), you still are not sure, go to the library for a few hours and do some research. A librarian will be happy to help you find current information about a particular subject.

The conclusion of this book puts our study of environmental backlash rhetoric into philosophical perspective. It reviews the language of money, the impact of beliefs on the collective unconscious, linguistic habits that hinder environmental discussions and a brief commentary on the potential impact of the backlash movement. Such philosophical aspects of language are important. In **Closing of the American Mind,** Allan Bloom agrees with many others who say the social crisis of the 20th century is really an intellectual crisis. "Our problems are so great and their sources so deep that to understand them we need philosophy more than ever." (Bloom, 1987, p. 6)

Presenting this material poses the risk that it might cause someone to distrust those who try to persuade them, or cause unnecessary skepticism. This would hinder the ability of people to understand environmental issues, not help it. In **Faces of the Enemy**, Sam Keen identifies mistrust as a cause of war. "The word paranoia is only the most recent name for this temptation to yield to a pervasive need of radical mistrust, defensiveness and cynicism." (Keen, 1991, p. 98) If this material causes the reader to be distrustful of a persuasive speaker's words, it will have missed its mark. Knowledge of persuasion strategies and the fallacies they could conceal should prevent, not encourage, an inclination to distrust.

P
A
R
T

O
N
E

The Red Flags

This section lists and defines the
language indicators that suggest the
possibility of fallacious reasoning.

RED FLAG TERMS*

Persuasive Words

1. Anecdotes, Stories and Metaphors
2. Double-Bind
3. Contingency
4. Rapport
5. Authority
6. Humor
7. Emotional Words
8. Pacing
9. Questions
10. Missing Words
11. Absolutes

Fallacies

12. Loaded Questions
13. Misrepresentation of References
14. After This, Therefore, Because of This
15. Circular Reasoning
16. Face Value
17. False Cause
18. Personal Attack
19. Burden of Proof
20. Either-Or
21. Generalization
22. Ignoring the Issue
23. Contradiction

Intent Signals

24. Us vs. Them
25. Supremacy
26. Absolute Certainty
27. Righteous Indignation
28. Intimidation
29. Affiliations

These terms are defined in this section. In Part Two, Rush Limbaugh's phrases illustrate how they are used. The numbers listed after each statement in Part Two refer to this page.

PERSUASIVE WORDS

Words cannot be remote from reality
when they create reality.
--John Cowper Powys

A rhetorically sensitive student of persuasion
can check such threats to a democratic society.
--Raymond Ross (Ross,1981)

An accomplished persuader knows how to use language to achieve his purpose. "Persuasive words" are his tools. Top salespeople, negotiators and trial lawyers use them regularly. Most do not fully understand how or why their words wield such power, but university research shows that certain kinds of language can significantly diminish a listener's critical thinking. (Herd, 1984)

This does not mean persuasive language can always overcome reason, nor allow someone to do something against his will. It can lower critical thinking, but it does not eliminate it entirely. Persuasive language merely triggers mental processes that have more to do with memory, imagery and emotion than with analytical thought. In extreme cases, however, the right combination of factors can result in deadly persuasion. If a captivating speaker convinces people that a particular action will ultimately

9

lead to a desired end, and if many other factors come into play, an event such as Jonestown might be possible, or, perhaps, a global equivalent.

To prevent being misled by such language, we must know when it is being used. With this awareness, our critical judgment stays sharp. We will then be sure to carefully consider the persuader's message before we think or act in a particular manner.

1. Anecdotes, Stories and Metaphors

Stories have been a vehicle for teaching and persuasion for thousands of years. They make people comfortable. After all, our parents told us stories when we were children. Story tellers weave ideas into a story so its characters come to the conclusions intended. By suggesting a likeness between the character and the listener, the speaker uses a powerful tool of persuasion, the metaphor. Stories stir emotions, create images, bypass critical thinking and motivate the listener to associate with or against the character. A story doesn't have to be long to accomplish its goal. For example, the following anecdote would have more persuasive power than a direct plea attempting to promote a "pro-life" viewpoint.

I met a young man named John recently at a pro-life meeting. He had just won an award for saving the life of a child who almost drowned in a lake. During our con-

versation, he told me his unmarried mother had considered an abortion before he was born, but had changed her mind at the last moment. The child's mother was also at the meeting. "I'm sure glad John was here to save my child," I heard her say to someone.

Single words and brief analogies can also trigger a metaphor. Telling a person he is "***burning*** his money up" is likely to prevent him from making a foolish purchase more than saying he "is better off not spending the money." Analogies like those below are equally effective.

"The early pioneers tamed a wilderness. Nothing was handed to them. And they sought only freedom and a better life for their children. Today, government is taking away our freedom and mortgaging with debt the future lives of our children." (Limbaugh, 1993, p.76)
Or,
"When the Serbs launched a genocidal scorched-earth policy against the Muslim population in Bosnia, it was characterized as "ethnic cleansing." Liberals are up to the same thing . . ." (p. 227)

In the following portion of a story about the Pilgrims, Limbaugh allows William Bradford to make his argument for him about the value of free enterprise:

"Bradford, who had become the new governor of the colony, recognized that this form of collectivism was as

costly and destructive to the Pilgrims as that first harsh winter, which had taken so many lives. He decided to take bold action. Bradford assigned a plot of land to each family to work and manage, thus turning loose the power of the marketplace." (Limbaugh, 1993, p.71)

2. Double-Bind

If you ask a friend, "Would you prefer a beer or a scotch?" chances are good he will have one or the other, even if he wants neither. Professional sales agents are taught to close a sale by asking the prospect, "Would you like us to install it on Monday or Tuesday?" or "Do you want to use my pen or yours to sign the agreement?" This kind of persuasive language represents a "double bind." Two alternatives are offered, both leading to a desired objective.

The double-bind strategy thus provides the receiver with an illusory freedom of choice between two possibilities, neither of which is really an option that has been carefully considered. The uncritical listener, for example, might choose one or both of the following choices, not conscious that he has demeaned the group represented by his choice.

I don't know who is worse, the environmental wackos or the feminazis!

Researchers are unsure why double-binds are so effective. On the surface, it seems we would recognize the trick, or would be more objective with our decision. They can and do work, however, as easily as when used with children. If we tell a child to go to bed at 8:00 P.M., he is likely to resist the order. If, however, we ask whether he wants to go to bed at 7:45 P.M. or 8:00 P.M., the majority will select the latter option of their own free will.

Double-binds are most enticing when the two alternatives are positive, but they can work when both are negative.

Which kind of liberal do you want in government-- the kind that sees the American people as incapable and tells them nothing, or the kind that thinks they are uninformed and lies to them?

In this example, a question turns an either-or fallacy into a double-bind device. If asked skillfully, this question could sway a person to become anti-liberal in his thinking, even if his better judgment had kept him unbiased previously. Double-binds take many forms. See if you can identify any in the following Limbaugh argument:

"Do you think all men are rapists? Do you think looking at someone is sexual harassment? Do you think all sex is rape? If your answer to any or all of these questions is no, you are simply not, by definition a feminist." (p.202)

3. Contingency

What do the following statements have in common?

- *While the President delivers his State of the Union speech, notice how many lies he tells.*

- *Unless you want America to become a third rate country, you must stop listening to the hysterical bleeding hearts that care more about Bambi than they do about people.*

- *Perhaps you are not courageous enough to see my point.*

- *If you really want to see a small, productive American city become a ghost town; if you really think trees are more important than human beings, sign the petition to close our lumber mill!*

All of the above sentences typify ways a speaker can link two ideas so they must be accepted or rejected together. If the listener identifies with the first idea, he is compelled to accept the second. Similarly, if he does not identify with the first, he is likely to reject the second as well. This is a common strategy used by persuaders.

4. Rapport

Creating an affinity with the listener is a prerequisite for effective communication. The following techniques are all ways a trained speaker uses persuasive words to build sufficient rapport.

(1) The first is a positive introduction. It should instill confidence and a sense of togetherness. Within the first few sentences, the listener ought to feel that the speaker is there to assist him. Such an introduction begins to reduce the defensive posture normally associated with meeting a stranger. Although body language and voice pitch cannot be detected when reading, Mr. Limbaugh none-the-less manages to obtain and maintain rapport with his readers. In his opening sentence in **See I Told You So**, he immediately relates to his audience as, "my friends." (Limbaugh, 1993, p. xiii) He continues to use this phrase frequently throughout his books and his broadcasts. In this book, he says, "my friends" or "folks" fifteen times in the first forty pages alone. It may seem trite, but it is efficacious. (President Clinton used a similar phrase, "My fellow Americans" five times in his sixty-three minute State of the Union Address in 1994.)

(2) Showing respect for the listener is another way to gain rapport. A real life anecdote shows how important this is. A firefighter, EMT, who took one of my workshops on effective patient communication, responded to a medical emergency the following day. A five year old girl had walked into a dog pen that housed six sled dogs. At first, they starting playing with her, but in a matter of moments the play got rough. Before she was rescued by her mother, she received several lacerations and puncture wounds. She also had a large avulsion on the back of her hand. When we arrived, the girl was screaming hysterically. Her parents and neighbors kept telling her she was "OK," but the young person paid no attention to them. The more they attempted to calm her down, the more she screamed and the more she bled. The medical technician approached the little girl and introduced himself, confidently, bending down and talking at her level. He then said, with sincerity, "Wow! Look at all that blood. I'll bet that really hurts, doesn't it?"

For the first time, the child responded. She nodded her head yes, and began to control her convulsive wailing. The EMT continued, "I'll bet all that good, red blood has cleaned the dirt out of your cuts and doesn't need to bleed anymore. You can make it stop by just holding this soft pad on your hand, while I put a bandage on your leg." The girl took the pad and the EMT said, "Good, look at how you are stopping the bleeding. Wow, you are really special!" The child stopped crying completely, and she stopped bleeding!

This true account, one of many that show the power of this kind of communication with trauma patients, started with the EMT showing respect for the little girl. He was the first person who acknowledged her fears, her pain and her tears. It was the first time she had ever seen her own blood, and he let her know that he knew what she was feeling. He continued showing respect, all the way through the treatment. Getting her to help hold the gauze pad, and telling her she was special, were all designed to do this. In his public persuasion efforts, Limbaugh seems to understand the importance of this strategy as well. Here are two examples:

"You are good people, decent people, and I knew you were fully capable of maintaining civility and order in your own community. " (Limbaugh, 1993, p.103)

"Who listens to me? The answer is obvious: all across the fruited plains, ordinary Americans of every walk of life listen. You know who you are--you are the ones who have the courage to face and believe the truth. You are the people who make the country work. " (p.22)

(3) Speaking the language of the listener also creates rapport. This, of course, includes speaking the same national language as the listener, although a trained person can develop rapport with body language during a one on one encounter. Essentially, though, this means identifying with the person or people the speaker wants to persuade. Anything that accomplishes this, such as using the local vernacular, will suffice. Even the rate of speaking can help a speaker identify with an audience. For example, the average high school educated audience prefers a speaker who talks around 170 words per minute. (Incidentally, Limbaugh speaks an average 177 words per minute, based on a sampling of three TV broadcasts.)

In the following quote, Limbaugh gains rapport by relating with those fellow Americans who know all to well the economic difficulties of the times:

"But don't think I am some kind of Polyanna. I have seen tough times as well. I've been on every rung of the socioeconomic ladder."

"I've been fired six times. I've been broke twice. I've been hopelessly in debt. I've gone through periods in which I made very little money. I've also been near the top. I've seen life from all sides." (Limbaugh, 1993, p. 9)

(4) Hopefulness builds rapport. Napoleon Bonaparte said a leader is a dealer in hope. This perfectly describes much of the success Limbaugh has had in building rapport with Americans.

"Don't believe the doomsayers. Don't believe the negativity-mongers. Don't believe the American-bashers--even if one of them is the president of the United States. Don't buy the lie that punishing high achievers will bring you happiness . . . This is still America and America is not over." (p. 33)

At a time when humans are being criticized for their behavior, especially regarding environmental degradation, Limbaugh's message is opportune. People prefer not to feel badly about their normal activities and lifestyles, and Limbaugh goes out of his way to make sure they do not. Many of his statements, like the one above, however, represent more than hope alone. They also portray cynicism. Hopeful messages that put positive images in our minds are good. Hopeful messages that distract attention from problems may not be. Hope should be joined with positive direction, not with cynical assaults on large groups of Americans who may not be motivated by self-interest. Kenneth Clark says, "We can destroy ourselves with cynicism and disillusion just as effectively as by bombs." Hope is an essential ingredient for ending disillusion, but so is love. Attaining positive rapport with one group at the expense of another group can ultimately lead to despair. And, *my friends*, despair is the opposite of hope.

5. Authority

The fallacy of appealing to an illegitimate authority can work because authorities in general have an advantage when it comes to using persuasive words. It is the trusted authority figure we obey when we are frightened or confused. The placebo effect in medicine, for instance, is largely due to the assumed authority of the physician. This allows his words to initiate healing by simply telling someone a sugar pill is real medicine. (Chopra, 1989, p.62)

The climax of Limbaugh's introduction brilliantly employs an indirect inference of authority by listing quotes of people such as Voltair, Thoreau, Paine, Virgil and other great thinkers. He follows this with a calculated humor, *"Isn't it amazing that these guys knew all this . . . without having to listen to me?"* (p. xvii)

This is just the beginning, however. Through Limbaugh's dialogue, he confirms and reconfirms his authority, using the extroverted *hubris* that is his trademark. Below are just a few samples of language that helps him maintain an image of authority.

"See, I told you so." (p. xvi)
"You are about to be exposed to the kind of bristling, cogent analysis available nowhere else . . . Don't fight it. Don't even try. Surrender yourself." (p. xvi)
"Many years ago, I compiled some of the most lucid observations the world has ever known in the form of "The Thirty-Five Undeniable Truths of Life." Every one of those insights has withstood the test of time." (p. 78)
*"I have been proved right about so many things since my first book was published that **See I Told You So** could easily have filled several volumes by simply cataloging such validations."* (p. 171)

6. Humor

Herbert Gardener said, "Once you get people laughing they are listening and you can tell them almost anything." Gardener's quote says it all about this aspect of persuasive language. Books have been written in the field of psychoneuroimmunology on the ability of humor to heal disease. Humor therapy has brought people out of depression, where clinical psychology was not successful. If someone has the ability to get a person to laugh, it will be easier for him to persuade that person to do something else.

This does not mean, of course, that persuasion should preclude humor. We should, however, see it as a red flag so we are not beguiled beyond the point of no return. We should be especially mindful when a speaker's humor is at the expense of another person or group. When this happens, the chances that a fallacy is in the making begin to increase.

7. Emotional Words

Many words have universally similar connotations. Words like "love" and "freedom" typically provoke positive feelings. "Pain" or "imprison" will produce negative ones. Advertisers know the universal responses to certain words. In his book, **Words That Sell**, Richard Baylan lists such words for every aspect of marketing a product, from the "grab" to the close. (Baylan, 1994) Politicians know many universally emotional words also. It would be difficult to persuade people to rally around a nationalistic platform, for example, without using words like flag, patriotism, freedom or America.

A persuader can be most successful with emotional words in person, when body language and expressive speech can be used to absorb a listener. However, the written word can be effective as well. In both cases, the result is a temporary suspension of critical thinking. Limbaugh, like most skilled persuaders, constantly uses emotional words in his oratory. Positive emotional words Limbaugh often uses to promote affirmative feelings and responses are listed below.

Hot, enormous, phenomenal, hottest, compassion, great, proud, flawless, American, hope, freedom, free enterprise, positive future, power, winning, truth, excellence, righteous, right, baby, humanity, our country, democracy.

Here are some negative emotional words Limbaugh uses to provoke cynical feelings and responses:

Hot air, dead wrong, enslave, doomsday, horrendous, staggering, frenzied, liar, communism, soaking the rich, gut-wrenching, astronomical, tyranny, insincere, radical, terror, dread, manipulate.

8. Pacing

Many of us have seen the television version of Perry Mason stand up in the courtroom and object because his rival was "leading the witness." Pacing strategies, mastered by lawyers, hypnotists, ministers and other professional persuaders, use subtle words and phrases to move a listener toward a desired viewpoint. They lead a person from a reference point to the destination intended by the speaker.

Generally, pacing begins with a provable or probable premise. Often, this simply means reiterating the beliefs or sentiments of the listener. If the listener agrees with the premise, he has taken the first step. If the speaker paces his audience correctly, the listener will take more steps. Word phrases which convince the listener a sentence is likely to be true are called pacing phrases. Here are some that Limbaugh uses when pacing his audience:

Let's face it . . .
Without question . . .
A well documented editorial . . .
I don't have to tell you again . . .
Let's be honest . . .
This is why . . .
To quote from an authority . . .
As an expert, I . . .
I'm not telling you anything you don't already know.

Don T. Jacobs

Once a speaker states a premise that is probably valid, he is ready to tie a less provable one to it:

To quote from an authority, dinosaurs became extinct without human intervention, and we all know humans are not at fault for any other animals environmentalists tell us are becoming extinct.

All that is necessary to pace someone into believing the second half of this sentence is a conjunction like "and," "but," "since," "while," "as" or "then." Let's look at the word, "but." It connects coordinate sentences or ideas. Coordinate means equal, as opposed to subordinate. So, by making a second statement, which may not be true, equal to the first statement, which is probably true, we are led to believe the validity of the second declaration. Observe this method of pacing in the following Limbaugh argument. It is broken into the three parts of a pacing progression that lead toward the desired objective.

(1) *"Some scientists are convinced that a number of early civilizations were brought down by environmental degradation of the land."* (This, most of us would agree, is probably true. It is even a position many environmentalists would agree with.)

(2) *"But as corrupting as any civilization may be to the environment, earth is remarkably adept at healing itself."*

Using the conjunction, "but," the idea that the earth can, on its own, remedy any havoc wreaked upon it by

24

civilization is now given as being equally valid to the first premise. No room is left for any reasonable counterarguments regarding the degree or duration of pollution, nor regarding the motivation of civilized man to fix things.

(3) *"Now, the real shocker. Human beings, operating in a capitalistic system, are better equipped to solve their own environmental problems, to clean up their own messes, than any other species operating under any other economic system. In other words, free markets are not incompatible with, but are essential to, environmental health."* (Limbaugh, 1993, p. 175)

"Now the real shocker" serves in this statement as the connecting phrase to tell the listener that capitalism can fix any environmental problem. Such a statement would normally require some qualifiers before being accepted. Under what condition would the responsibility be assumed? Would regulations or laws be necessary? Could the problem be too pervasive or costly for after-the-fact resolution?

To achieve the final destination of Limbaugh's persuasion objective, he uses the classic equalizing connector, *"In other words."* This time, we are told to believe that free, unrestrained technology is "essential" to environmental health. (Limbaugh uses such conjunctive pacing devices continually. In his recent book, he begins a paragraph with "But" fifty-six times, compared to using "I" twenty-nine times and "The" thirty-one times.)

Repetition is another pacing strategy commonly used by Limbaugh and other people who influence public opinion. It is the technique people often think hypnotists use to induce hypnosis. Say something often enough and in as many ways as possible, and soon listeners begin to accept your message. Limbaugh has used this strategy with name calling. Some people who have frequently heard him refer to environmentalists as "wackos" may have come to regard environmentalists with more depreciation than before. Limbaugh is quite open about his use of repetition:

"What have I told you over and over about the role of the military? What have I explained countless times.? But, perhaps most important, what have I told you about the environmental movement? What have I said it's really about? What have I told you over and over again?" (p. 172)

9. Questions

When used by a rhetorician, a question can become a persuasion technique. With it, a speaker can sway someone in three ways. First, questions can make it seem that the intent of the speaker was the listener's own idea. "Would you like to sit down?" really means, "Please sit down", especially if a chair is pulled out and a gesture suggesting its use is made. Similarly, the therapist who asks his patient, "Can you tell me about your childhood?" and then waits intently for an answer, will probably hear a life history.

The second persuasive effect of a question relates to its ability to temporarily confuse the person being asked it. If the question is not an easy one to answer, or if it is asked quickly, the listener's mind becomes anxious while he searches for a respectable reply. At this point, the speaker answers his own question, much to the relief of the listener. In this vulnerable moment, the listener is more likely to accept the answer than if it had been presented initially as a simple declaration.

Lastly, a question can have a suggestion or an assumption embedded in it. If an automobile salesman asks a casual shopper, "Why do you want a new car?" he has embedded the idea the shopper indeed wants a new car. The customer might reply, "Well, the old one is getting a little worn, but we are just looking because we don't have much money." The salesman replies with another question. "About how much could you afford to pay if we could get you into a new car today?" At this point, the skillful salesman has control, all because of his adroit understanding of the power of the interrogative.

Salespeople become so proficient at using questions, a good one is easy to spot during almost any conversation because of his use of questions. The person who asks the question leads the listener and controls the discussion. To say Limbaugh also uses questions routinely would be an understatement. In his recent book, nearly 300 of the 353 pages contain at least one question in it. Furthermore, they are used to achieve one of the three persuasion objectives. In the following quotes from Limbaugh, an unproven assumption, often a generalization fallacy, is embedded within the question.

"Why are liberals so reluctant to engage in open debate?" (Limbaugh, 1993, p. 237)

"How could so many people be fooled so badly?" (Limbaugh, 1-22-94)

"Why did we allow liberalism to poison our nation's soul?" (Limbaugh, 1993, p. 76)

"Why is it that every environmental wacko thinks that the solution to all so-called environmental problems is for you to change your lifestyle?" (Limbaugh, T.V. Broadcast, 1-24-94)

The following are just a few examples of how Limbaugh asks questions so he may give the answer:

"What does that mean? That we shouldn't attach too much meaning to his words? Exactly, my good friends. Point made." (Limbaugh, 1993, p. 216)

"Why are these issues so important? Why are they worth fighting for? Because if there are no ultimate standards of behavior that descend from God . . . then life itself has lost its meaning." (p.83)

"Why do they react that way? They take offense because deep down they know they're wrong." (Limbaugh, 12-23-93)

10. Missing Words

Like questions, certain words also cause the mind to search for meaning. In linguistics, such words are called comparatives. The majority end with the suffix "er" or "ly". They tend to prompt the question, "compared to what?" In other words, if we hear a speaker say the word, "Clearly," our brains search for a meaning by asking, "Clearly, compared to what?" Here too the persuader can assist by guiding the listener where he wants. The listener, however, is more inclined to search his own world view for a satisfactory answer. (Moine, 1990, p.92) By so doing, he eventually agrees that the verb described by the adverb, "clearly," is, at least, more *clear* than *something* that is *less clear*. This gives him a reference point, vague as it may be. We apparently need such perspective when we are communicating. Inadvertently, it also gives some validity to the speaker's sentence that contains the adverb. This is why it is used so recurrently by persuaders, even if they have no idea how or why such words tend to encourage agreement.

Here are some missing word phrases Limbaugh has used. Notice how the addition of the adverb enhances the credibility of what is going to be stated, even without knowing the rest of the sentence.

> *"As is flawlessly illustrated..."* (Limbaugh, 1992, p. 131)
> *"Their goal is simply not to allow..."* (Limbaugh, 1-94)
> *"Simply put..."* (Limbaugh, 1993, p. 139)
> *"Clearly, the answer to that question is no."* (p.259)
> *"If you wish, you may simply ignore..."* (p.24)
> *"It simply boils down to this..."* (p.169)
> *"Then, gradually, there was a shift..."* (p.190)
> *"Unfortunately, feminism another of those..."* (p.187)
> *"Finally, after reversing..."* (p. 180)

11. Absolutes

The science of General Semantics teaches its students that any premise using an "allness" statement, as when using the words "always" or "never," will result in a fallacy. None-the-less, such statements can make for powerful persuasion when spoken with authority to a vulnerable listener. They convey finality and stifle further discussion. In hypnosis they are the hypnotic suggestions. In sales, they are the closes. Although not required to make an absolute statement, key words like "don't" and "must" help insinuate an absolute premise into the listener's mind. Such words are frequently used by Limbaugh to form absolutes:

> *"Even if you reject the Bible as the Word of God, you must still admit . . . "(Limbaugh, 1992, p. 105)*
> *"Don't ever forget . . ."(Limbaugh, 1993, p. 261)*
> *"But don't forget . . ." (p. 294)*
> *"You must overcome the presumption . . ." (p.287)*
> *"The answer is an emphatic, "No" . . ." (p. 131)*
> *"Make no mistake . . ." (p.40)*
> *"Don't believe . . ." (p. 33)*
> *"We must respect the system . . ." (p. 219)*

There are few manners of speech more persuasive than a seemingly indisputable declaration from a confident orator. Imagine the vocal inflection and body language of Limbaugh, speaking the following words he wrote in his book:

> *"In this chapter I will present factual, documented, undeniable, take-it-to-the-bank proof that the 1980s have been totally and intentionally mischaracterized by slick liberal politicians with the active complicity of the mainstream establishment media." (p. 111)*

This kind of preface to an argument parallels the persuasive effort of a trial lawyer giving his opening statements to the jury. An important difference, however, is that the jury is *supposed* to be objective. This is their primary function. The people on a jury are also given instructions regarding objectivity. If one lawyer appeals to emotions or uses fallacies, an objection is raised immediately. The average listener may not always be as critical of a media personality.

The absolute directive or suggestion is the finale of a persuasive argument. If it follows the correct sequence of linguistic strategies (which, interestingly, is also the classical structure of hypnosis) the chances are good it will be successful:

1. Hold the listener's attention
2. Start with ideas that are difficult or impossible to disagree with.
3. Increase the need for a listener to respond and look forward to what is going to be said next.
4. Give clear directions about where you want the listener to go next.

In **Patient Communication for First Responders: The First Hour of Trauma**, (Jacobs, 1990) I provided a mnemonic to help readers remember the essential components which lead to a convincing directive that could influence the emergency victim's survival and recovery. They are the same as those that make persuasion effective, so I offer it here as well:

"CREDIBLE"

Confidence (Project confidence.)

Rapport (Develop Rapport.)

Expectations (Build positive expectations.)

Directives (Give definite suggestions.)

Imagery (Directives should evoke images.)

Believable (Directives should *appear* believable.)

Literal (When we are hyper-suggistible, words may be interpreted literally, so beware of what words are used.)

Enthusiasm (Directives should be given with the right amount of enthusiasm.)

Now that we have an understanding of how persuasive language can lead us to believe false statements as easily as it can cause us to believe true ones, we will next learn how fallacious reasoning often points us in the wrong direction as well.

FALLACIES

Nothing can now be believed which is seen in the newspaper. Truth itself becomes suspicious by being part of that polluted vehicle.
--Thomas Jefferson

Man, the timid seeker of truth, wishing so desperately to be accepted, will listen to any folly.
-- Ramtha

(Nomenclature for the fallacies that follow is traditionally in Latin. To simplify learning, I have used the English translations to name them. For example, it may be easier to remember and understand "after this, therefore because of this" than "post hoc ergo propter hoc.")

Simply put, a fallacy is a misleading argument. Aristotle is credited for classifying fallacies. He wanted his students to know, in any given case, the available means of persuasion. He, and Plato as well, had observed the misuses of the art of persuasion. Both contributed to the science of logic to prevent such misuse. (Ehringer, 1974, p. 45)

34

During the past twenty-five hundred years, many other great thinkers have attempted to reduce the use of fallacious persuasion. Locke, Bacon, Spinoza, Leibnitz, and Kant are among those who wrote volumes on the subject. Some thought Aristotle overemphasized deduction. Others criticized his "allness" premise, claiming it too often led to false generalizations. (Korzybski, 1933) Many, following the lead of Stephen Toulmin, suggested that a logical study of moral language had to include an understanding of qualifiers, which allowed for exceptions, qualifications or reservations. (Toulmin, 1964)

This section on logical fallacies omits rather than adds information to the abundant literature on logic. It devotes little space to syllogisms or enthymemes, and provides only a cursory look at the formal rules of logic. We do not concern ourselves with inductive versus deductive reasoning. Nor will we criticize a particular academic school of thought regarding the structure of logic. I have neglected these things to make it easier to learn how to carry out "the social imperative to become sensitive and knowledgeable about persuasion." (Ross, 1981, p.5)

An interesting consideration, although not too important, is if Rush Limbaugh himself is an erudite student of logical persuasion and fallacies. It may be more important to know if he uses fallacious arguments intentionally or not. We will see from our analysis of "intent signals" in the following section that his primary motive for communicating may be to persuade. (See also

"Throughout the book you will be challenged, because you will actually be persuaded to the conservative point of view." (Limbaugh, 1992, p. xiv) There are some indications that he knows something about the art and science of logic, and that he intentionally designs some of his fallacies. If this is true, he may be guilty of sophistical reasoning, or the deliberate use of a fallacy to persuade others to agree with one's opinion.

There are several things that suggest Limbaugh uses sophisms in his statements. He is, for example, familiar with fallacy terminology. Of course, many intelligent individuals with a good vocabulary could know the nomenclature of logic. None-the-less, when combined with other observations about his language and intent, it is fair to consider the possibility he may intentionally use fallacious reasoning in an effort to persuade. The following statements reveal his knowledge of the vocabulary of logic.

" Just keep a sharp eye out and be prepared to combat their propaganda, sophistry, and history revision with the truth." (Limbaugh, 1993, p. xv)

He also uses terms, such as, "fallacious premise," "ad hominem," and "non-sequitur" fairly frequently in his criticism of others:

"This means that the media must be accountable and responsible to and for itself, which we all know is a fallacious premise at best.") (Limbaugh, 1992, p.271)

" There is a fallacious premise out there that black kids have low self-esteem because they don't have any roots." (p. 206)

"On March 27, 1992, he launched a blistering political and ad hominem (i.e., personal, for those of you in Rio Linda, California) attack on President Bush's Haitan policy . . . " (p. 42)

"At first glance, such a non sequitur rings true with most good people." (p.58)

"Why do they so often resort to ad hominem attacks and name calling?" (Limbaugh, 1993, p.237)

Limbaugh answers the question posed in this last example with, *"Because they are unable to win the arguments on their merits."* (p. 237) His recognition that name calling is inappropriate is admirable. (As we will see, name calling is a classic propaganda tactic, besides being a fallacy listed by Aristotle twenty-five hundred years ago. It is also a violation of the advertising code of American business to be "disparaging against competitors.") (Newsom, 1976, pp. 265-93) It is worth noting Limbaugh's double standard here, however. For example,

Don T. Jacobs

on the very next page, Limbaugh calls President Clinton's brother "half-witted".(Limbaugh, 1993, p. 239) In fact, Limbaugh uses *ad hominem* attacks, with labels such as "communist," "environmental wacko," "feminazi," "liberal elitist," "phoney," etc., frequently throughout his radio, T.V. and published commentary.

Psychology teaches that accusations against others often reflect things we know about ourselves. For instance, when Limbaugh says, *"Environmentalists are consumed with egocentricity,"* or, *"They manipulate words skillfully to convince the public,"*(Limbaugh, 1993, p. 215) this might suggest he is wrestling with related issues himself. The contradiction between his prolific practice of insulting others, and his professed desire to refrain from personal attacks, could indicate a possible inner conflict. In **Toxic Faith**, the authors explain that "Underneath the raging ego of a persecuting leader is a suffering person who fears being unimportant." (Arterburn, 1991, p.170) They go on to say that such a leader emerges because "a driven personality accompanies tremendous talent and charisma," and that the more popular he becomes, the more license he takes in his oratory. Limbaugh himself admits his early tendency to attack others was inappropriate and that he learned not to continue with the practice. The fact that he still does may give some credence to the inner struggle described above.

"Realizing that I was allowing my talents to be exploited toward destructive ends, I decided to change

38

course. I resolved to make a detailed study of the me-dia--especially the personalities, like Johnny Carson, who had longevity in show business. None of them insulted people . . . This study was an eye-opener for me. And it gave me something to think about." (Limbaugh, 1993, p. 31)

Another sign that Limbaugh practices sophistic reasoning is his ability to construct logical syllogisms. Many of his persuasive arguments are perfectly structured syllogisms. That he can do this without training or intent is possible, but it may also result from expertise. Limbaugh freely admits such expertise in the chapter from, **See I Told you So**, he titles, "Lies are Facts; Facts are Lies."

"Without question, presentation, packaging, imaging and superficiality are all extremely relevant in the political world . . . As an expert in both form and content--in both delivery and substance . . ." (1993, p. 286)

Let's analyze the structure of the following argument.

"Rights are either God-given or evolve out of the democratic process. Most rights are based on the ability of people to agree on a social contract, the ability to make and keep agreements. Animals cannot possibly reach such an agreement with other creatures. They cannot respect anyone else's rights. Therefore they cannot be said to have rights." (Limbaugh, 1992, p. 104)

39

Breaking this down into its syllogistic form, we find a perfect syllogism, i.e., a structure of inference that combines two premises so as to cause a consequential conclusion.

(1) Rights are based on the ability of people to keep agreements.
(2) Animals cannot possibly make agreements.
(3) Therefore, animals cannot be said to have rights.

Furthermore, his syllogism meets all eight rules that formally govern the science of logic:

1. Only three terms can appear, a major (no rights), a minor (animals) and a middle (agreements).
2. A universal conclusion must follow a universal premise. (It does.)
3. The middle term (agreements) cannot occur in the conclusion. (It doesn't.)
4. The middle term must be used in both premises. (It is.)
5. If both premises are affirmative, the conclusion must also be. (No violations here.)
6. Both premises cannot be negative. (They are not.)
7. If one premise is negative (animals cannot keep agreements), the conclusion must be negative (Therefore animals cannot have rights). (Both are negative.)
8. One premise must be universal. (It is.) (Bittle, 1950)

We must keep in mind that syllogisms, even when in correct form and when following the formal rules, are

not necessarily true. Their validity is based on the soundness of the premises. In other words, the logic can be
sound even if the premise is in error. Also, the ability to
argue with perfect syllogisms does not prove conscious
knowledge of their use any more than using a fallacious
argument proves someone is intentionally being illogical to gain an advantage. Our question regarding
Limbaugh's intentions, considering the possible evidence, are none-the-less legitimate.

Whether Limbaugh is guilty of sophistic reasoning
or he is unintentionally fallacious remains an open question, and one the reader can investigate further when we
discuss "intent signals." In either case, it is the listener's
responsibility to find out if a persuader's arguments are
valid or not. To be objective, however, requires awareness of another persuasion strategy that definitely un-
derlies many of Limbaugh's statements. It is known as
ad populum, or appeals to a preferred viewpoint of the
public.

*" What accounts for the unprecedented popularity of
my words . . . ? 'Finally! Here's someone saying what I
think' is the most often heard reaction people have when
they are exposed to my ruminations. "* (Limbaugh, 1993,
p. xiv)

The psychology of "non-contradictory behavior"
(Jacobs, 1981, p. 143) and dissonance theory (Festinger,
1957) explain that our search for comfort and consistency

between how we act and how we think is a strong motivating force behind our convictions. We generally try to avoid facing our contradictions. When we are aware of one, it "undercuts our convictions and kills our capacity to be certain of anything." (Jacobs, 1981, p.139) During a time when the media and the environmental groups are making us aware of our ecological and environmental imprudence, behavior that might contradict our higher values, we are drawn toward "knowledge" about the environment that reduces dissonance. This is the knowledge Mr. Limbaugh provides to us. Therefore, as we look for the following fallacies in statements, we should be aware of our own tendency to *hear no evil, speak no evil and see no evil.*

12. Loaded Questions

By asking a question in which the speaker has included an unproven assumption, loaded questions can trick a person into accepting a false premise. For example:

Have you ended your radical appeals to the senator about groundwater pollution?

If you answer yes or no to the essential question regarding communication with the senator, you have admitted that your appeals were radical. This is an admission that could later be used against you. In this illustration, using just one sentence, the loaded question is fairly obvious. The strategy is more subtle when many questions are skillfully combined to lead the listener to a fallacious conclusion. When this happens, the combination of answers can create the same dilemma for the person being persuaded. Observe how this is done in the following argument.

We know the groundwater is cleaner now than before, don't we? And isn't it true that recent water clean- up was funded by our organization? How can you argue that environmentalists, who are increasing your taxes, can be effective in managing the costs of new clean water legislation? Isn't it reasonable that you stop your futile efforts and take a more sensible approach by signing this petition?

Loaded question fallacies assume that many premises are true, but present no evidence to support their validity. Sometimes, instead of a question, a statement can be loaded with one or two words that make unproven assumptions, as in the following:

It is my purpose to show that these immoral environmentalists, who are destroying private property, should immediately be thrown out of town when they come in to demonstrate today.

In this statement, the entire proposition may be fallacious if there is no evidence that the environmentalists in question are actually destroying private property or are immoral. If these accusations are not questioned, however, it will seem appropriate to stop them from demonstrating in the town.

13. Misrepresentation of References

Intentionally quoting statements out of context, and using statistics deceptively are the two most common misrepresentations of references. (Of course, blatant misquoting may also result in a false conclusion.) The context within which a statement is made often defines its true intention. Without it, we can interpret words to mean the exact opposite of their original meaning. In the following paragraph, if the third sentence were quoted alone, the person being quoted could become known for a position quite different from the one he truly holds.

Everyone on the planet is responsible for preventing overpopulation. Those whose economic situation precludes a healthy environment for their offspring must be especially aware of this responsibility. I believe married couples in the United States should have the right to decide how many children they want. However, I believe their decision should be based on thoughtful consideration of their own economic situation.

If I wanted to use this person's speech to support a position that there should be no restriction on people's rights to have as many children as they want, I would merely need to use his third sentence alone.

(Limbaugh quotes out of context quite often, as will be illustrated in Part Two. For a condensed illustration, see his seven page summary of quotes he attributes to President Clinton. (Limbaugh, 1993, pp. 46-52) This kind of overkill and personal attack is antienergistic to Limbaugh's own purported goals for America. Even if the President has not yet lived up to many of his campaign promises, criticism of this possibility should not be relegated to such a hostile format.)

Statistics can also mislead us. A well-known expression reminds us of this: "First come lies, then big lies, then statistics." Statistics that relate to life span, for instance, may show that people live longer because of improved medical care for adults, while another set of statistics might show it is only because of decreases in infant mortality. If a speaker uses statistics to make his argument, question them carefully before accepting his conclusion. If the statistics "prove" there are more trees now than ever before, ask what area the statistics cover or what kind of trees were surveyed. If a persuader uses statistics to say that white Americans never practiced genocide against Native Americans by showing there are more Indians alive today than in 1492, ask how many were alive in 1870. (See Part Two.)

14. After This, Therefore, Because of This.

Superstitions are the classic illustration of this one. You blame a black cat which walked in front of your car for an accident that happened sometime afterwards. Persuaders, however, use more subtle versions of this fallacy. All that is necessary is to misuse the sequence of events as they relate to time as in the following illustration.

More small businesses have collapsed since the publication of Al Gore's book on the environmental crisis than ever before. His prophecies of doom have caused people to stop investing capital in companies. People are afraid the customers won't buy products that aren't considered "ecologically safe."

If presented eloquently, the possibility there is no relationship between Gore's book and statistics that suggesting an increase in small business failures may go unnoticed.

15. Circular Reasoning

When a fallacy results from circular reasoning it is because the speaker has combined unproven statements to prove a particular proposition. Here are some illustrations:

Organic agriculture should not become widespread or it will cause worldwide starvation. Such a tragedy would result from any policy that tries to stop the use of pesticides.

In essence, the two sentences above prove each other by saying, "Pesticides cause world starvation. Starvation, therefore, results from the use of pesticides. Here are two more examples of circular reasoning.

• *Listening to the rhetoric of Paul Ehrilich is a waste of time because nothing he has predicted about overpopulation has come true. The predictions about overpopulation didn't come true because they came from Paul Ehrlich.*
• *Environmentalism should be stopped because it causes undue panic. We know it causes unnecessary alarm because it should be stopped.*

As ridiculous as such logic appears when we look at it closely, it is remarkable how often persuaders use it successfully.

16. Face Value

This fallacy describes an irrational appeal to get us to believe what a person says is fact. Persuaders use this when they want to intimidate or bully us into accepting what they say at face value (See "Intimidation" under "Intent Signals").

Environmentalists, of course, have caused the over-regulation of business. Before the onslaught of liberal ideology, unregulated free enterprise brought this nation to its greatness. This is why our country leads every other country in the world in life span, health care, education, income, safety on the streets, and freedom.

Although this speech states several fallacious conclusions, (We are not ahead of all other countries in these things. See p.119) a forceful speaker might easily convince people to swallow his entire message.

Another way a speaker can use this fallacy is if he bases his argument on the words of a supposed authority who is not legitimately associated with the subject matter. If Michael Jackson is used to support a contention that the rain forests should be saved, it would be best not to take such supportive evidence at face value.

17. False Cause

This fallacy results from a premise that assumes something is true because of something else which is not. Because the strategy is almost as confusing as this definition, it often slips by a listener without notice. Here is an example of false cause reasoning:

The AIDS virus, caused by homosexual activity, is bringing attention to the Gay community. Health care research in heart disease should become a new priority because it relates to the entire population.

Here, the inference that only homosexual activity causes AIDS might fool someone into accepting the conclusion that heart disease should become the new priority. Let's say an individual was arrested for drunk driving in a small community. Let's also say an arsonist burned down the church the same day. In reality, there is no connection between the driver and the fire, but an enemy of the drunk driver wants to blame him for the crime. At a town meeting, he announces, "Authorities arrested the person, who caused the fire, for drunk driving." A listener may not initially challenge the assumption that the person who was arrested for drunk driving also caused the fire. If later in the speech, however, the speaker blames the drunk driver directly for starting the fire, and wants revenge for it, he might successfully convince the listener who failed to challenge the assumption initially.

18. Personal Attack

As mentioned earlier, this fallacy is also called *ad hominem*. It occurs when one is drawn to a false conclusion because a proponent of the counter argument has been successfully discredited by the speaker. (Comparably, one can discredit an opponent by accusing him of believing something he truly does not believe.) This strategy is more subtle than name calling, but is equally unethical. By convincing us the major spokesperson for a particular agenda is a "bad" person, we may be encouraged to reject this person's entire platform. Below is one of Limbaugh's favorite personal attacks for a single act of "hypocricy" that he uses to discredit the larger picture.

"Didn't Tom Cruise make a stock-car movie in which he destroyed thirty-five cars, burned thousands of gallons of gasoline, and wasted dozens of tires? 'Tom, most people don't own thirty-five cars in their life. Now your're telling other people not to pollute the planet?' Shut up, sir." (Limbaugh, 1992, p.159)

Since most individuals make mistakes, or occasionally act in contradiction to their philosophy, it is easy to find a transgression to attack, even if it is an exception to the rule. It would be a fallacy to generalize a conclusion based on a personal attack against someone for such an isolated action.

19. Burden of Proof

This fallacy occurs when a speaker asserts his premise as being valid until someone proves otherwise. Such a requirement may or may not be necessary to prove the premise false. Study the following two opposing views.

View One: *The storage of radioactive waste in the ocean may not be safe because it is likely the metal containers will rust out within 50 years, according to preliminary research.*

View Two: *There is no conclusive evidence that a metal can, submerged at 300 feet, will actually deteriorate within 50 years. Our cans have lasted 10 years without any obvious damage. Until someone proves us wrong, we will stay with our policy of storing radioactive waste.*

In view number two, the speaker may win the debate by having shifted the burden of proof onto the people who have the first view, even if the current policy probably is not the best solution.

Burden of proof fallacies are difficult to spot because a requirement for proof is often essential before a new viewpoint is accepted. One criticism of the environmentalists has been that they expect actions to be taken even if there is not irrefutable scientific proof. They prefer to err on the side of safety, rather than risk irreversible repercussions for the sake of temporary economic setbacks that could have tragic local significance on individual lifestyles. This is a challenging issue and can probably only be resolved by a case by case discussion on the potential benefits and risks of a particular action.

In 1976, I wrote a book exposing the need for improving the physical fitness of American fire fighters.

This profession is the most hazardous occupation in the U.S., owing to heart attack mortality rates considered to be job related. (Jacobs, 1981) At that time, the relationship between cardiovascular fitness and heart disease was not medically conclusive. Legal concerns and a variety of political considerations caused much opposition to the idea of in-house fitness programs (in spite of the evidence that showed the duty of a fire fighter could be compromised if he had an unnecessary heart attack on the way up a staircase to save a child.) The grounds of the opposition rested with the burden of proof fallacy. There was not *positive* proof relating heart attacks to the athletic job requirements of an individual who was 60 pounds over fat, smoked two packs of cigarettes a day, and had a very low aerobic capacity. Fifteen years later, the NPFA finally published a national standard to implement the book's message. How many lives were lost because the information and the opportunities for its application were stalled? Again, the logic of scientific probability was overcome by the excuse of scientific absolutism.

20. Either-Or

This fault exists when a contention with more than two possible alternatives is presented as if there were only two alternatives. We often see this fallacy when "us v. them" labels are used, such as, environmentalism vs. free enterprise, religion vs. science, liberal vs. conservative, etc. When a speaker condenses a problem that has many opportunities for resolution into an either this or that context, he only impedes a real solution. In the following portrayal, there are obviously other alternatives to consider. However, when presented expertly, amid a deluge of oratory, the audience could easily find themselves making a choice between only the two propositions. In the following example, neither choice is valid, but too often a speaker will get someone to choose anyway.

You must decide now. Either you want America to become socialistic, and therefore endorse the environmental movement's proposal to ban all automobiles that get less than 25 mpg, or you must vote to end all automobile regulation.

21. Generalization (Sampling and Extrapolation)

The basic generalization fallacy simply uses "all" or "none" to win an argument. "All liberals have more concern for animals than for humans" is an obvious generalization. The most dangerous aspect of this kind of fallacy is that it usually starts with provable facts. The preceding sentence, to be effective, would have followed an accurate description of a self-proposed liberal who really said he was more concerned about animals than humans. The fallacy occurs when this sampling is used to generalize a more pervasive picture.

Another way to generalize into a fallacy is to extrapolate a few known or provable things into a statement about the future that really cannot be predicted from these things. This is what happens in the following agument:

Robert Malthus was wrong about his prediction that overpopulation would become a crisis by 1900. Paul Ehrlich was wrong about his predictions regarding overpopulation reaching a crisis point by 1990. Any doomsayer that says we will have a population crisis in the 21st century is an extremist we would all be better off to ignore!

Generalizations come in all shapes and from all levels of intelligence. A professor concluded an article about environmental extremism, recently published in *Reason*, with the following statements:

" Their moral fervor runs parallel with high education and not a little dedication. After all, the most notorious mass murderer of our century came from the culture of Mozart and Goethe, favored animal rights, and was a fastidious vegetarian." (Benford, 1994,p. 41)

Generalizations can sometimes insult one's intelligence. Someone once defined advertising as "the science of arresting human intelligence long enough to get money from it." Substitute "intelligence" for "awareness", and the definition may not be so far from correct. At the airport recently I noticed a huge sign sponsored by the Sugar Association, Inc. that read:

"After an extensive three year FDA study, the government gives sugar a clean bill of health. All the things you wanted to believe about sugar are true, and the government has confirmed them. The FDA has confirmed that sugar is not the cause of obesity. . . "

Besides being a very narrow interpretation of the actual study, human intelligence or awareness would indeed have to be temporarily "arrested" to believe that sugar does not relate to obesity. Certainly sugar is not *the* cause of obesity. Like any other food that has calories, it is only *a* cause of obesity. If you eat too much of it relative to other foods, however, it could become *the* cause. "All the things you wanted to believe . . . and the government has confirmed them" seduces us into believing a conclusion that, although might make us happy, is irrational.

To help prevent such generalizations, make sure the samples are relevant, and if there are a reasonable number of them. Find out if they are objective, and if they cover a critical period of time or location. Like Josh Billings says, *"It ain't so much what folks don't know, it's what they know that ain't so."*

22. Ignoring the Issue

A motion picture entitled, "The Ballad of Gregorio Cortez" exemplifies this fallacy. (I must ad-lib a little, for it has been years since I have seen the film.) In it, a man named Gregorio defends himself against an attack from two others who just raped Gregorio's wife. One of the two draws a gun in the skirmish, accidentally shoots his partner instead of Gregorio. He then runs away and tells the sheriff that Gregorio did the killing.

Gregorio is arrested and goes to trial. At the trial, the evidence is strongly in favor of Gregorio. He has a capable lawyer who manages to bring forth this evidence. The attorney for the killer, however, continually ignores the vital issues. Instead, he reminds the jury of how peaceful the town was before Gregorio arrived. He points to the children of the dead man, and tells the jury to imagine how difficult it will be for them to grow up without a father.

The prosecuting attorney goes on eloquently about "apparently relevant, but objectively irrelevant" (Ross, 1981, p.173) arguments trying to cloud the evidence in Gregorio's defense. In this story, said to be true, the judge sentences Gregorio to death, and he is executed the next day.

The reader should note that an "ignoring the issue" fallacy often uses several other fallacies to accomplish its purpose. For examples, a personal attack on someone, appeals to the emotions and beliefs of the audience, and reference to an unrelated authority figure are all ways to ignore an issue.

23. Contradiction

A speaker might begin his speech with this sentence:

My friends, human beings are as important to God as are all of his other creatures. We are all together on this planet, and each living thing has a right to its freedom.

Later, he might say:

God created man in his image. He did not create animals in his image. Human progress should not be stifled because of some snail that is no more than an inch long!

If such an apparent contradiction is noticed, the listener should see it as a red flag showing that something may be amiss with the ultimate logic of an argument. When a speaker contradicts himself, it is usually because he is using whatever rhetoric will work at the moment to stir the appropriate emotions of his listeners.

More often than not, such contradictions will not occur within the same paragraph. Sometimes, they will not happen in the same speech. To become aware of the latter situation, the listener would have to be familiar with the speaker's previous statements, and take note of those that contradict one another.

Intent Signals

The aim of an orator is to convince us
he is not an orator.

--George Will

The intention of the speaker influences the accuracy of the information. A speaker is more likely to misinform if his purpose is self-serving. This does not mean selfish motivations are wrong or immoral. There is nothing wrong with using persuasion to make money, provide a service, or win votes. Too much self-serving motivation, however, has the potential of compromising integrity.

In most arts, the more obvious the intention, the less likely is the possibility of achieving the intent. Effective persuasion may hide self-serving objectives. A trained speaker can do this intentionally, but he might also be unaware of his own hidden agendas. When a persuader does not realize that the enthusiasm behind his belief represents some psychological condition, he can be especially convincing. In either case, listening for intent signals in a speaker's language can give clues to his real purpose. Although this book does not presume to know the intentions of Rush Limbaugh, his statements do influence the views of many people. It is, therefore, worth looking for such clues in his comments. We can begin by reviewing the intentions he has openly stated.

"I decided to write this book to tell a bit about myself and my radio show and where I stand on the important political issues effecting our society today." (Limbaugh, 1992, p.1)

"I thought my task would be to remember all the marvelous and wonderful things I had said in the past, organize them, and put them on paper. There was some of that, but what really propelled me was the discovery of things I had not thought of or realized before, new analogies, different ways to be persuasive on a point." (p.4)

These lines from the Introduction of his first book, **The Way Things Ought to Be**, seem to reveal a strong desire to be right, to win and to be recognized. The very title of his second book, **See, I Told You So**, suggests the same objectives. In the Introduction of this book he describes his reasons for writing it. He says the most important one was; *"I realized early on just how right I have been about so much."* (Limbaugh, 1993,p.xiv) I am not necessarily suggesting wanting others to know we are right is an unhealthy motive for persuasion. I am saying that we should study such statements to understand a speaker's true intention.

Besides his personal desire to persuade others that he is right, Limbaugh also seems opposed to journalists who are more objective than he is. He implies their purpose should be to make their listeners happy:

"Remember this above all else: My success is not determined by who wins elections, my success is determined by how many listeners I have." (Limbaugh, 1992, p. 22)

"One of the things that has always bothered me about people in the media is that they pretend they aren't in a

business. They think they work for a public service. That is why so many of them don't care if the customers are happy or not." (Limbaugh, 1992, p.271)

His criticism of journalistic objectivity is also apparent in his attacks on the "Media". For example, he criticized CNN correspondent, Bernard Shaw for "not taking sides." He was upset because, according to him, Shaw did not want to give the government certain information about his coverage of the Gulf war because he felt it would compromise his integrity and neutrality as a journalist. (p.272)

Some people think Limbaugh's intent is strictly to entertain, that his statements are primarily satire, and that he is only having fun. This does not appear to be the case. Limbaugh himself writes:

"You may be wondering if this means that I don't really care about my beliefs, that I am simply using them to attract like-minded people. Wrong-o. To the contrary, they are my heart and soul, the essence of my being, and I never betray them or misrepresent them in the pursuit of audience, other than when I am doing satire and parody. I am quite aware that millions of people invest their trust in my honesty, and I will not ever be cavalier about that." (1992, p.22)

And:

"New York culture critic David Hinckley wrote a column recently in which he stated: 'The thing with Rush Limbaugh's fans is they don't know he's kidding.' I suspect that like so many other liberals, he just can't believe that my message is sincere." (Limbaugh, 1993, p.17)

Don T. Jacobs

Understanding Rush Limbaugh's or any other persuader's intentions will help us decide if further research is necessary. Self-serving motives are red flags that should encourage such inquiry. When they appear, it may be consequential to ignore them. George Gordon's dedication in his classic text on persuasion emphasizes this possibility:

"This book is dedicated to the many millions of people who, throughout the ages and up to the present, have been persuaded to death." (Gordon,1972)

24. Us vs. Them

A definition of a liberal is 'a muddleheaded idealist who rejects time honored values for the sake of remedying temporary social ills' tells more about the prejudices of the person offering the definition that it does about the meaning of the term "liberal".
--Douglas Ehringer (1974,p.45)

If a speaker's attitude, body language, intonations, voice inflections or words imply that an opposing view belongs to an "enemy", consider carefully the validity of his statements. Although it is natural for human beings to want to identify with a group (The teenage gang epidemic is an extreme example of this tendency), this desire should not be the driving force behind an argument. To a point, it is healthy for mind and spirit to share a common system of beliefs with a particular group. The dividing line between these points occurs when the group sees someone as a threat to their affiliation. When this happens, arguments promoting various issues may have more to do with validating the group's identity than putting forth a truth. It then becomes more important to view any statement in terms of which side its spokesperson is on, than in terms of its merits.

Historically, "Us vs. Them" language has been most apparent in war and religion. The need for it in war is obvious, but makes little sense in religion. Considering that theologians define "Christ" as "Truth" (Fox, 1979, p.85), defense of a religious affiliation without concern for the truth is a paradox. "The mark of true atheism is not a theoretical disbelief in a being called 'God', but the actual centering of one's existence around the enemy," says theologian turned philosopher, Sam Keen. (Keen, 1991,p.100) As moral fervor becomes more of a part of the environmental debate, it will be increasingly important to watch for the "Us vs. Them" red flag if we are to detect actual priorities.

"Us vs. Them" language is usually easy to identify. It frequently uses words such as "they, them, their, our and us." It will also involve the labeling of opponents of the speaker's position, with such terms as "capitalist, socialist, environmentalist (and environmentalist whacko), left, right, liberal, conservative, etc. Frequent use of any words showing a bias against "an enemy" warn of the possibility that the speaker's statements may not be well founded.

In the environmental arena, the most obvious language of enmity relates to the labeling of people as liberals or conservatives. Since the linguistic implications of these terms are so deeply rooted in the environmental debate, it is worth taking a few minutes to see the inappropriateness, if not the irony, of putting people into such ideological categories.

Many books have been written which attempt to describe the ideologies of liberalism and conservatism. Some blame conservative "psychology" for paving the road to fascism.(Wilson, 1973) (Adorno,1950) Others blame unlimited liberalism for doing the same thing. (Spraeger, 1981) Webster's Dictionary defines a fascist movement as a "movement toward nationalism and conservatism, as opposed to internationalism and radicalism." (5th ed, 1946.p.364) This brand of government, which opposes all radical elements, ultimately leads to the autocratic authority of some charismatic leader. This, of course, is something neither liberals nor conservatives want.Yet, it is the clash between the factions identifying with each camp that sets the stage for tyranny. Following is a brief description of how the so-called liberals and conservatives mutually create the problem they both want to avoid. Assumptions assigned to each group swing the pendulum of accusation from one extreme to the other until the momentum is too great to slow it down. This "ping pong" phenomenon works something like this:

Liberal: Man imagines "heaven on earth", then attempts to create various utopias.

Conservative: This effort is radical. Perfection is not possible for man on earth. Reality is not so heavenly. Free enterprise offers the next best thing to heaven -- wealth.

Liberal: The attainment of wealth is associated with suppression of individual rights of workers. Counter efforts include laws to restrain free enterprise.

Conservative: The efforts to restrain free enterprise is associated with suppression of individual rights of entrepreneurs. Counter-efforts include public criticism of law makers who are thought to be responsible for such suppression.

Liberal: People retaliate against the criticism of law makers by appealing to ideal values relating to global responsibility and individual dignity. Retaliation becomes more radical. Individualism degenerates into irresponsible subjectivism.

Conservative: Leaders convince masses of the futility of governmental efforts to achieve utopian ideals. They focus on the increasing social insecurity and frustration that result from the social and political battle that exists. People become confused over issues of morality and choose sides. The human tendency toward militarism, punishment and ethno-centrism fosters anarchy.

Anarchy is the parent of tyranny. When people become confused and desperate, they are more willing to follow an authoritarian personality. The banner of traditional values hides the arbitrary and despotic exercise of power of the new leader. People will now follow orders more readily. They no longer try to find out what is propaganda and what is truth.

It is thus the "Us vs. Them" rhetoric that defines liberal and conservative attitudes. It polarizes different viewpoints and puts people against each other. The language of liberalism and conservatism causes people to forget they must work together to achieve their goals, which ultimately are not that dissimilar. When looking for "Us vs. Them" signals, remember most propaganda efforts feed on sentiments which already exist. Their intent is not to establish new attitudes, but to manipulate those that surround the current issues. (MacDougal, 1966,p.93) In his article, *The Analysis of Propaganda: A Clinical Summary,* (Lee, 1945,p.37) Alfred Lee lists the universal techniques of propaganda. As you will see, most of them include "Us vs. Them" strategies:

- Selecting a crucial public issue to escalate social competition

66

- Simplifying issues for slogans and other sayings that emphasizes being on the right side of the competition
- Name calling
- Transferring something prestigious onto the side of one's position
- Using testimonials of famous people to support one side of the argument
- Implying that the position is on the side of "plain folks"
- Getting people to join the "band wagon", not the "queer outsiders"
- Using specific damaging information to discredit the opposition
- "Cardstacking"
- Generalities

As you listen to both sides of the environmental debate (and, of course, as you read Limbaugh's statements), see if you can detect language that illustrates such propaganda strategies. If you can, the next step is to make sure the information being given is accurate and will support an objective platform designed to encourage cooperative change.

Dr. Neal Barnard, President of "Physicians Committee for Responsible Medicine" sums up the "Us vs. Them" problem in "The Psychology of Abuse": *"This sort of "good vs. bad", "us vs. them" thinking leads to the use of preference, rather than morally relevant criteria, as a basis for ethical decisions."* (Barnard, 1991, p. 51)

25. Supremacy

*The quest to become a superman, rests upon
the fear that I am less than human.*
-- Sam Keen

Professional communicators know to keep "I, me,
mine" to a minimum when speaking or writing. "Be
interested, not interesting" is a phrase taught in many
salesmanship training seminars. A persuader who reveals too much self-appreciation during a presentation
may lose his audience. His purpose becomes suspect,
even if his message is true.

Of course, there are exceptions. If a person's claims
consistently prove valid, we may forgive a degree of
self-centered language. Sometimes, especially in sports
and entertainment, a personality benefits from his self-
aggrandizing behavior. Mohammed Ali's pomposity
ultimately increased his popularity. Fans also expect
certain Hollywood movie stars to maintain an air of supremacy.

When people try to persuade us, however, we
should pay close attention when we are told the
speaker, his product, his team or his ideologies are far
superior to others, (even if the claim ultimately proves
true). There is nothing wrong with such an assertion
per se. It can suggest, though, the possibility that the

need to assure supremacy is stronger than the desire to impart accurate information. If someone truly believes the slogan attributed to Vince Lombardi, "Winning isn't everything; it's the only thing," there is a chance he will say whatever is necessary to win the listener's confidence. (As I write this, a news report came over the radio describing a physical attack on an ice skater, apparently intended to prevent her from competing against a rival during the Olympic trials.)

Modern civilization has elevated the importance of being "#1" to extreme proportions. The countermovement, however, may be riding the pendulum too far in the opposite direction. The result is either avoidance of competition, mixed feelings about it, or both.

Rush Limbaugh has recognized the growing fear and/or resentment of competition, but his language may be contributing to the problem. On one of his television shows (Dec.,1993), he carried on about a football game that ended in a tie, explaining how frustrated everyone involved, players, referees, media, spectators, etc., must have been. In his second book, he accuses the National Football League of "constantly striving for parity." (Limbaugh, 1993, p.13) He says this is part of the liberal movement's relentless pursuit of equality that is ruining America. (pp.12-15) He says, "*Competition has become a dirty word among liberals in our society.*" (p.13) His own understanding of competition, however, may be throwing on the dirt.

If there is a growing negative attitude about competition in our culture, and there does seem to be, it is found between liberals and conservatives alike. The fallout from the overly advertised idea that "winning is the only thing" has caused Americans of every political and ideological persuasion to put down competition, rather than be victimized by it. The language of supremacy in competition, not competition itself, is what they are really trying to avoid. Many youthful athletes, driven by parents, coaches or culture to be "number one" have found themselves in therapy, or worse, because this rhetoric taught them that performance at a given time is equal to self-worth. A tied football game should not be a disappointment if both teams played skillfully and aggressively to the best of their abilities. To believe otherwise is the very antithesis of the original Olympic creed: "It's not whether you win or lose that is important, but how you play the game."

This language of supremacy and winning at any cost has no place in a proper discussion of environmental issues. Competition can be useful here if we define it as a race toward excellence, not supremacy. When this occurs, competition then can provide free enterprise with an incentive to discover new ways to improve the environment. When competition is no longer associated with supremacy, it is a wonderful way for both *sides* to test the effectiveness of training and ideas.

26. Absolute Certainty

*The end of the human race will be
that it will eventually die of civilization.*
-- Ralph Waldo Emerson

By definition, absolute knowledge does not come from scientific inquiry or broad-based research. It is determined in itself. It has no qualifiers or conditions. It cannot be challenged or vetoed. The person who professes to be absolutely positive about something will entertain no doubt. He will consider no questions.

If a persuader is so absolutely certain about his conclusions, chances are he has based his information more on faith than on facts. Although faith may be able to move mountains, it alone may not be sufficent to save them. In a discussion about the environment, it is best if we make important decisions with reason as well.

Scientific methodology itself builds on probability, not absolutes. If a particular outcome holds true through enough experiments, it becomes a working hypothesis or a theorem. Surrounded by one set of conditions, a proven theory can be depended upon. Introduce a new condition, however, and the original theory may no longer be valid. Since scientists cannot predict all the combinations of conditions that may come into the picture, they are rightfully reluctant to predict an absolute result under all circumstances.

The history of progress has been a continual dance between those who have been absolutely certain and those who have confronted this certainty with new or opposing ideas. The first seekers of a truth pay a price for such an assault on the absolute knowledge of the times. "You can always tell a pioneer by the arrows in his back," goes the old saw. The dance, however, goes on, as it should. If defenders of the status quo changed beliefs too easily each time a new hypothesis came upon the scene, civilization would be more chaotic than it already is. On the other hand, if old knowledge is not continually investigated, civilization could stagnate or allow vital errors to become permanent.

This dance, however, has become more dangerous today than ever before. The power, the rapidity and the global effects of technology have increased the urgency of the music. More information. More knowledge. More power. More fear. The status quoers and the changers are becoming reluctant to do the dance together, as the radical moves of one threaten those of the other. As Allan Bloom says in **Closing of the American Mind**, "The gravity of our given task is great, and it is very much in doubt how the future will judge our stewardship." (Bloom, 1987,p.382)

In **Faith and Reason**, Richard Swineburne explains, "Nothing will count as a belief unless it is compatible with the way in which the believer seeks to realize his purposes." (Swineburne,1981, p.18) In other words, we tend to remain absolutely certain about those beliefs we are accustomed to. For example, if a person writes books to earn respect, he will not accept a belief that says book writers are not respectable. The more emotional investment he has made in writing books, the stronger will be his resolve against hearing the opposing argument. Even if he is open-minded enough to listen, someone must convince him that he can readily attain his purpose another way. "Belief is relative to the alternatives." (p.18)

Many statements on both sides of the environmental debate will show the "absolute certainty" red flag. If unquestionable resolve, rather than reasonable assurance, is behind a conviction, check it out before buying it.

27. Righteous Indignation

Hatred is self punishment.
--Hosea Ballou

A spokesperson for one of the large environmental groups was reported to have said, "Ultimately, our cause

73

will win because truth is on our side." He then proceeded to vent his anger on the people who apparently retaliated against his organization's efforts to stop lumbering in a particular region. If this person offered data to support his position, a wise listener would regard it carefully. When someone is so full of guiltless virtue and vengeance because of "unjust treatment," his information is likely to be biased and inaccurate. Ultimately, this could hurt a worthy cause. Admittedly, what is truth and what is worthy are difficult things to know. But if this is not appreciated by a persuader, it could indicate he has taken an easy path to his position. It shows he may not have carefully analyzed his assertions. It is not likely he has open-mindedly compared his ideas to other viewpoints. The listener should thus question his information.

Righteous indignation blinds us to the mutuality that exists among all people when it comes to environmental issues. People consumed by it eventually find themselves drowning in a pool of selfish emotions. There is an ancient story that reveals how quickly and easily such a person can kill what really is important to himself and others.(Estes, 1993) The story is about a king who has returned to his castle from fighting at war. He is anxious to see his son, who was born while he was away. As he approaches the castle, his loyal and beloved dog romps out to greet him. But something is wrong. The dog has blood on his lips and tongue. His hair is matted thick with it. Furthermore, the animal does not meet his master head on, but acts peculiar and runs into the baby boy's room. The king follows the great dog and, to his horror, sees the cradle toppled over and the room smeared with blood. In a rage, he draws his sword and kills the dog. Then, a moment after, he hears the baby cry. He looks beyond the cradle and sees the baby, uninjured, lying next to a large, dead wolf that had entered the baby's room. The dog had killed it in order to protect the king's son.

When a persuader raises his sword of indignation, remember that the object of his scorn may really be the hero.

28. Intimidation

The passion for truth is silenced by answers
which have the weight of undisputed authority.
--Paul Tillich

Until relatively recent times, most hypnotists used authoritative techniques to induce hypnosis in their subjects. Even today, a more intimidating approach produces trance quicker than a less threatening one. This may be because, as children, we became accustomed to doing what an authority figure told us to do, or else. Many top salesman also inspire their prospects with the intimidating power of their wit, their sarcasm, their quick and overbearing retorts. Their use of strategies can make a prospect feel badly if he doesn't agree with the salesman. Intimidation strategies can be direct or indirect. Look for subtle signs of coercion in the speaker's intonation, body language and in phrases like, "Can't you see?", or "I'm sure you are smart enough to agree," or "Whether you can admit this in the end will be a true test of your mettle as a human being." (Limbaugh, 1992, p. xiv) If the words are not overtly offensive, you'll be surprised at how readily you find yourself agreeing with ideas you might otherwise have challenged.

If a speaker employs intimidating techniques or uses words that inspire agreement for fear of ridicule, it is possible that his information will not stand on its own. Before letting someone intimidate you with such techniques, be courageous enough to investigate his ideas.

29. Affiliations

> *He never chooses an opinion, he just wears*
> *whatever happens to be in style.*
> -- Leo Tolstoy

The basic thing we want to understand about affiliations is that they come with agendas. Whether a fraternity (or sorority), a library club or the Klu Klux

Clan, most affiliations expect some degree of allegiance from their members. Furthermore, most members feel a need to do for their group, even if this only means sending a check once in a while.

Affiliations would not be red flags if groups were not as politically partisan as they often are. If a speaker is representing his group, or is being sponsored by it, the political agenda is likely to influence his intention. This does not necessarily mean the politics of a group are dishonest, excessively biased or spiritually evil. It would be unfair to accuse many groups, such as Amnesty International, the Cousteau Society or the Young Republicans, as being rebellious, or of being a threat to free enterprise or the environment. Many such organizations have a sincere concern for justice, dignity and freedom. These groups make every effort to present material that is well documented. We should not accept exhortations that are associated with an affiliation, however, without at least making sure they are objective. If we do not know if a speaker is affiliated with a special interest group or sponsor, it may be worth finding out. (To learn what affiliations your legislator may have, call 1-800-622-SMART.)

This ends **Part One**. In **Part Two** we will identify red flags in twenty-two arguments Rush Limbaugh has used to persuade us to accept his position in the environmental debate. The crux of each argument is recorded verbatim. In reducing his rhetoric to these primary sentences, I have tried to maintain the context he intended.

Since the purpose of red flags is to warn us of possible fallacies, I have responded to most by offering specific evidence that may refute premises and conclusions the flags challenge. In other instances, I leave it to the reader to decide on the logic and validity of a particular contention Limbaugh arrives at via persuasive words, fallacious reasoning or questionable intent.

Note: As a matter of sytle, Limbaugh's statements are presented in italics. They are printed in the same font size as the majority of the text and are not indented. Quotation marks are placed before and after each paragraph, for in some instances the paragraphs were not consecutive in the original text. Whatever rules of style I have broken are intended to improve clarity.

Television stars should be regarded as experts only in being television stars.
--Michael Fumento
(Fumento,1993)

Every new adjustment is a crisis in self-esteem.
--Eric Hoffer

P A R T   T W O

Misleading Statements from Rush Limbaugh

The following statements are direct quotes from Rush Limbaugh on matters relating to the environmental debate. Immediately after each statement, a list of numbers tell the reader which red flags appear in it. Refer back to the Red Flag list on page two if you want to test your ability to identify them. A critical analysis of the statement follows the numbers which describes the red flags in detail. When a particular one is named, it is highlighted in bold type.

Don T. Jacobs

Rushing the Animals

*A world in which man is not the darling of the gods, but
only another albeit extraordinary creature, is by no means
congenial to immature or wishful thinkers. But unless most of us
enter into the world to which Darwin opened the door, the future
of mankind is dim if indeed it has a future at all.*
--Edgar Cayce (Cayce, 1987)

*"The mastery of nature is vainly believed to be
an adequate substitute for self mastery."*
--Reinhold Niebuhr

This section begins with an analysis of Rush Limbaugh's
statements about animals. They represent an important part
of the environmental debate, and reflect much of the backlash rhetoric. The relationship between the environment and
a concern for animals should be obvious. The biggest threat
to the survival of the earth's wildlife is the destruction of its
habitat. (Jenkins, 1984) Directly and indirectly, this is
deleterious for the human population as well. Not addressing possible moral or aesthetic aspects of the wilderness
and its creatures, destruction of wildlife habit usually relates to a loss of a variety of resources advantageous to humans such as raw material for medicines. It also indicates
increased development and the harmful externalities this can
bring. The rate of extermination of mammals alone has in-

creased more than fifty-five fold in the past 150 years (McClung, 1986, p.16). If our own future is tied to the decreasing lifespan of animal species, we should study the kind of backlash rhetoric exemplified on the following pages before accepting it.

1. Primary Species

"One woman called my show to protest that animals do at least have one right: to kindness. I told her she was mistaken. Look at what they do to each other. They tear each other limb from limb. Humans do that too, but it's not the accepted norm. We accord ourselves redress for such wrongs. Animals don't think about right and wrong. They exist in the anarchical state of nature: survival of the fittest. When I suggested to my dog that animals had rights, he laughed out loud. To this day I don't think he respects me the way he did before I had that conversation with him."

"Human beings are the primary species on this planet. Animals and everything else are subspecies whose position on the planet is subordinate to that of humans."

"Humans have a responsibility toward lower species and must treat them humanely. Humanely, now that's an interesting term. Doesn't that mean as a human would like to be treated? Why not treat them animally? Because that would mean killing them. Can't you see? That's my point exactly." (Limbaugh, 1992, p. 106)

Red Flags:
1,3,6,7,8,9,10,15,23,24,28

This argument begins with an anecdote that also paces the listener from a provable premise to a possibly fallacious conclusion. A woman probably did call Limbaugh's show, and he most likely told her she was mistaken. From this point forward, however, he begins his decline into conjecture. This begins with a **generalization**. First, not all animals tear one another apart. Mostly carnivors do this. Second, he says animals live in an "anarchical state of nature." This infers a social group without order, a definition that applies to very few animal species.

Use of the sentences, *"Look what they do to each other."* and *"They tear each other limb from limb."* employs **emotional words** to evoke imagery and bypass critical thinking. After seeing such brutal images, we may be more inclined to accept the idea that animals have no rights. Limbaugh concedes that *"humans do that too"*, but dismisses it as not being the norm. (Notice that there is also no imagery association with this brief disclaimer.) Consider the validity of this dismissal, however. Is war a *normal* part of man's existence? If so, we know war results in man blowing apart his fellows at the rate of two wars a year somewhere in the world. On the other hand, if we say potential brutality against other humans is not normal, then we should ask if butchering pigs, cows, turkeys and chickens is normal. We, of course, tear limbs off other animals to eat them. If so, how is this significantly different than what animals do?

Limbaugh uses **humor** with his reference to his dog. As we chuckle at the idea of a dog "laughing out loud" during a "conversation" with its master, Limbaugh hits the listener with an absolute declaration. He tells us, *"Human beings are the primary species."* He reinforces this premise with two **questions** he first poses, then answers. Furthermore, the questions contain "ly" words, thus applying the **missing word** strategy. *"Humanely, as compared to what?"* is the question we ask ourselves when we hear the word, "humanely." *"As compared to anarchical animals tearing each other apart,"* is Limbaugh's reply.

There is a hint of **righteous indignation** here, as well as a tone of **supremacy** in the intention. Limbaugh seems slightly disdainful of the possibility that anyone could suggest an animal was not completely subordinate to man. He speaks as though the idea is an offense against his personal dignity, or against man's guiltless virtue. His tag question, *"Can't you see?"* even **intimidates** us into thinking this way if we want to be equally worthy. *"That's my point exactly"* takes us off the hook, and let's us know we came to the correct conclusion if we agreed, which he assumes we did.

We also have some **circular reasoning** and **contingency** persuasion in this statement. Animals are not humane because humane things are not animals, he tells us. Humans are not animal-like, because animal-like behavior is not like human behavior. Added to this circular reasoning is the contingency that if we treat others *"animally,"* this would automatically *"mean killing them."*

The use of the phrase, "survival of the fittest," presents a possible **contradiction** as well. As noted in Part One, we often can recognize contractions only when we compare a speaker's ideas with those he has stated at another time. For future reference, note here the negative connotation Limbaugh attaches to this Darwinian concept, as well as to anarchy. Find out if this conflicts with his attitude about free enterprise or about winning. See if entitlements and communism fit into the category of "survival of the fittest" and how Limbaugh's views on them correspond to his use of the phrase to demean animals. As for his negative feelings about anarchy, keep in mind his platform regarding government, and his vocal attacks on the administration. Anarchism, in human terms, is the theory that government is evil and that social organizations should be based on free agreements. The point is, if a persuader uses a concept in a negative way to support one argument and in a positive way to support another, such inconsistency may help reveal a more specific fallacy in one or both of the arguments.

Limbaugh's insistence that the difference between human and non-human animals are more important than the similarities, and that animals, therefore, must be confined to a category completely distinct from our own, is a concept for which the phrase "speciestic dualism" was coined. Embodied with the demand is the belief that the dominant way is always the superior way (in spite of Limbaugh's put down of "survival of the fittest".)

Dixie Lee Ray, author of **Trashing the Planet**, also reveals this kind of supremacy when she says, "It is demeaning beyond all belief to consider mankind simply as another species of animal." (Ray, 1990) Certainly we are special, but "demeaning beyond all belief" to just consider Darwin's theories seems an extreme position for the author to take. People who believe so strongly in "specieistic dualism" often seem to resent being made to feel guilty about environmental degradation. Dixie Ray was probably a kind, sensitive and caring person, like many others, including Mr. Limbaugh, who hold such fundamentalist attitudes. They would probably feel guilty about man's treatment of animals, if animals were interpreted with a higher regard. It is easier on their conscience to merely not have such a high regard for them.

A need to avoid guilt can stem from a fundamentalist belief that guilt means sin, and that sin requires punishment. The only problem with this philosophy is that unless we realize that we are not without guilt, we will not be motivated to fix the problems that face us. Whatever side of the environmental debate we are on, until we understand that we are part of the problem, we will continue to act irrationally. Kenneth Burke, in his treatise on persuasion, explains that transference of guilt often takes place through a variety of symbols, claims and actions. This, according to Burke, includes such verbal acts as "invective and name calling." (Fisher, 1970, p. 25-35)

One way to accept the fact that human behavior is a part of the challenges that face us, without feeling painfully guilty, is to redefine the word "guilt" itself. In her book, **Nature of Personal Reality,** Jane Roberts differentiates between "religious guilt" and "natural guilt." (Roberts, 1974) Natural guilt emphasizes prevention rather than punishment. It doesn't require spending one's life feeling bad about a transgression. It only helps assure that the transgression is not repeated. Perhaps if this understanding of guilt replaced the more widely accepted version, the language of the environmental debate would take an entirely new direction.

2. Dominion

"My views on the environment are rooted in my belief in Creation." (Limbaugh, 1992 p. 153)
"There is no escaping the connection between secular humanism and animal rights activism." The Bible teaches that God created man in His own image

and that He placed him on this earth in a position supe-
rior to all other creatures, and gave him dominion over
animals and nature." (Limbaugh, 1992, p. 105)

Red Flags:
11,13,16,23,24,25,26,29

There is little persuasive langauge in the above statements, with the exception of the absolute phrase, *"There*
is no escaping." There are, however, numerous intent
signals, punctuated by **absolute** language that says we
should take the argument at **face value.** There is also
possible **misrepresentation** of a reference, in this case,
the Bible. Such red flags warn us the argument may be
fallacious.

Many of Limbaugh's arguments regarding animals
rights and environmentalism are based on his linguistic interpretation of the Bible. In the above statements,
he clearly admits this. Since the foundation for his
viewpoint on these matters is a belief in the inerrancy
of the Scriptures, it is worth investigating the language
of the Scriptures themselves. Before entering this dangerous territory, however, a linguistic **contradiction**
regarding his claim that secular humanism is connected
with animal rights activism should be investigated.

"There is no escaping the connection between
secular humanism and animal rights activism."

Although the more obvious signal here is the "absolute certainty" red flag (*There is no escaping...*), charg-
ing animal rights activists with secular humanism is in-
herently illogical by definition. "Secular", according to
Webster's, means not under church control, not sacred,
or not spiritual. "Humanism" is a "mode of thought or
action centering upon distinctly human interests or ideals." Even if it were conceded that a high regard and deep
concern for animals does not involve a spiritual or sacred perspective (which I am not ready to personally concede), how could a concern for preserving wildlife be a
"distinctly human interest," especially when it is con-
trasted to Limbaugh's political and theological position
that human interests should be the primary focus of humans because humans are the primary focus of God?

*"The Bible teaches that God created man and...gave
him dominion over animals and nature."*

Limbaugh correctly paraphrases this teaching of the
Bible. In Genesis, man is given "dominion over every
living thing that moveth upon the earth."(*The Holy Bible*,
Revised 1953) This could possibly support Limbaugh's
argument if the word, "dominion", was indeed the one
chosen by God to describe man's relationship with animals. We should look carefully at the language before
making this determination.

In *The Earth in Balance*, Al Gore argues that "dominion" means something different than "domination" when
he tries to overcome the Creationist rationale for human
supremacy over nature. (Gore, 1992, p. 242) Semanti-

cally, however, the two words really do not infer different meanings. They both relate to supreme authority and jurisdictional control. In fact, when the Old English word "dominion" was originally used to translate the Scriptures from Hebrew and Greek (in the 17th Century), dominion meant "danger of being subject to the jurisdiction of." (Shiply, 1985, p.123) **The Dictionary of Word Origins** also explains that the early derivation of the word, "dominion," showed how subjects feared their overlords during a time when such power spelled danger to those beneath it. (p.124)

These new definitions bring us to the question, "Did God intend for man, the overlord, to spell danger for animals, man's subjects?" If we answer in the affirmative because the Bible tells us so (now that we know the definition and derivation of the word, "dominion"), we should reflect on whether or not this answer really "resonates with the higher truth" we discussed in the introduction. We should also ask ourselves if the answer is reasonable. Although Gore may have made an error in using a linguistic argument to show that domination over animals was not God's intent, his numerous references to teachings from religious leaders from around the world did give credibility to his conclusion. These esteemed individuals seem to have a different sense of God's intent for man's relationship with other creatures on Earth. For example:

"The world is green and beautiful, and God has appointed you his stewards over it."--The Profit Mohammed (stewardship implies "management" rather than "domination.")

*"As I have already stated, the seriousness of the eco-
logical issue lays bare the depth of man's moral crisis.
Respect for life and for the dignity of the human person
extends also to the rest of creation."* Pope John Paul II
(Pope John Paul, 1990)

The man who first translated the Bible into English,
William Tyndale, may have chosen the word "dominion"
because it reflected the attitude of 17th century Europeans
about what is referred to in modern times as "animal rights"?
Many of those who read Tyndale's translation accused him
of willfully perverting the meaning of the Scriptures, and
even burned him at the stake for it. Yet, in spite of this, his
work became the foundation of subsequent English versions?
(The Holy Bible, 1953, Preface) With this understanding of
the history of the langauge of the Scriptures that Limbaugh
uses to assert his position, it is reasonable to challenge his
position without challenging one's faith in the wisdom of
the Bible. Perhaps such an argument, based on a single word
written long ago in another language by an unknown author, may not be strong enough to use as an excuse for the
extinction of a species. It also seems sensible to be more
critical of a speaker whose message is based solely on the
word Mr. Tyndale chose to represent what God intended
man's relationship with animals to be.

According to a 1991 direct translation of the original
Greek version of the Gospel, According to John, we are
told:

In the beginning was the Word, and the Word was toward God and God was what the Word was. It was with God in the beginning. All things happened through it, and not one thing that happened, happened without it. Within it there was Life and the Life was the light of the world. And in the darkness, the light is shining... (Gaus, 1991, p.9)

This interpretation may tell us more about human dominion over the world and our relationship with the earth and its creatures than any other. Words, and the laws and commands they represent, are responsible for how we see the world and react to it. The original power of the word is as great as ever, only now it is spoken through the lips of many profits. For this reason, those who use words to persuade others to follow some truth or another, should do so with responsibility and care.

3. Only a Moron

"Rights are either God given or evolve out of the democratic process. Most rights are based on the ability of people to agree on a social contract, and the ability to make and keep agreements. Animals cannot possibly reach such an agreement with other creatures. They cannot respect anyone else's rights. Therefore, they cannot be said to have such rights."

"Thomas Jefferson, in drafting the Declaration of

Independence, did not begin by saying . . . "All animals are created equal. Webster defines a "right" as "something to which one has a just claim. The power of privilege to which one is justly entitled. Notice these words, one, person, another. All of these words denote human beings, not animals, or any other creatures. Implicit in all these dictionary definitions is that in order to have rights one must know that he has a just claim to them; one must be able to assert them. Only a moron would argue that an animal has the capacity to answer a claim to any rights." (Limbaugh, 1992, p. 104-105)

Red Flags:
2, 5, 10, 11, 20, 23

As we noted in Part One, this particular argument represents an almost perfect syllogism. There are nine red flags, however, that warn us the premises themselves may be faulty. Four of these are persuasive word signals. There is an appeal to a respected **authority** figure, Thomas Jefferson. The use of his name is fallacious because Jefferson's wording of the Declaration of Independence had little to do with the issue of animal rights. A **missing word** device, employing an "ly" word, is also used in the phrase, "cannot possibly." This reinforces the phrase's contribution to the **absolute** conviction that the entire statement is true.

The fourth persuasive words technique, a **double-bind,** is built into the **either-or** proposition in the first sentence. Although most either-or-fallacies cause one to choose opposing viewpoints, in this case the use of a double bind causes whichever choice you make to lead you to where Limbaugh wants you to go. *"Rights are either God given, or they evolve out of the democratic process."* What is interesting about this combined use of a double bind and an either-or statement is Limbaugh's bold assumption that the first alternative, the possibility that rights are God given, absolutely means that only man has rights. He doesn't try to support this assumption. Rather, all his evidence is behind the "democratic process" rationale. This, it would seem, is for good reason, since the first reason is logically indefensible. If we agree that rights are God given, it would be easy to make the argument that God *might* have given rights to animals, since even Limbaugh would admit that all creatures are in God's domain. In fact, Limbaugh's own preferred resource might make the argument for us. In the biblical passage describing God giving Noah lordship over animals, God also promises never again to destroy the earth. He seals this promise, using a covenant with man and every living thing on the earth. "When the bow is in the clouds, I will see it and remember the everlasting covenant between God and all living creatures, all the flesh that is on the earth."(Genesis 9:8-17) It would appear, accordingly, that animals were indeed regarded as being capable of entering into an agreement!

Immediately following the either-or choice, Limbaugh gives us a **generalization**. He says, *"Most* *rights are based on the ability to agree on a social contract.*" This, however, may **contradict** the first choice he offered, that rights could instead be God given.

To support his argument, Limbaugh attempts to use semantics, an excellent idea if one uses the correct meaning of the words he addresses. Limbaugh, however, makes several semantic errors. He uses Webster's defintion of "right" as "something to which one has a just claim" and as "power of existence to which one has a natural claim." He should have taken a moment to look up "just" and "natural," as both definitions would cause the meanings he quotes to throw the concept of rights back into the realm of God and all of his creatures. Webster says "natural" means "in accordance with the nature of its kind" and "just" means "righteous, especially before God."

To further embarrass the semantic justification for his position, he tells us to notice that words like "one" *"denotes human beings, not animals, or any other creatures."* Once again, Webster's Dictionary does not agree. It defines "one" as "any person or thing unspecified." I thus believe we could use the word "one" to refer to an animal. For example, if you asked me if I have seen any elk lately, I might answer, "Why yes, I saw *one* yesterday."

The majority of the intent signals identifiable in this argument reveal the familiar **supremacy** concept. To help assure the listener agrees with mankind's exclusive right to having rights, Limbaugh concludes his argument with an intent to intimidate. *"Only a moron would argue that an animal has the capacity to assert a claim to any rights."* By using the word, "assert", Limbaugh may be literally correct. The obvious inference, however, is that only a moron would argue that an animal has rights. At the risk of being so labeled, I must say I believe such an argument could easily be made just using the evidence exposed in our brief analysis.

4. Twaddle

"This twaddle has even crept into science reporting. The New York Times reported . . . dolphin's behavior and enormous brains suggest an intelligence approaching that of human beings or even, some might argue, surpassing."

"I was offended by that. Could somebody please show me one hospital built by a dolphin? Could someone show me one automobile invented by a dolphin?" (1992, p.109)

Red Flags:
27, 19, 15, 20, 25, 28

Any argument that includes mention of one's dignity being personally offended waves the **righteous indignation** red flag and tells us the possibility of fallacious reasoning is in the making. There seems to be a growing body of research connected to the subject of dolphin intelligence. Much of it points to the possibility that their intelligence might parallel that of ours. To insinuate that an idea is ridiculous because it is personally insulting is to admit that the grounds for an argument are purely emotional.

The three logic fallacies woven into this oratory are **circular reasoning, burden of proof** and **either-or** fallacies. The circular argument implies dolphins can't be as intelligent as humans because they can't invent automobiles or build highways. The circle comes back on itself with the idea that we know they can't do these things because they are not as intelligent as man.

The **either-or** problem tells us that dolphins either can invent automobiles and build highways, or they are not intelligent. This premise is validated with the **burden of proof** fallacy posed by the two **questions** he ends the argument with: *"Could somebody show me one highway built by a dolphin? Could someone show me one automobile invented by a dolphin?"* In other words, until someone can, the premise remains true that the possibility of dolphin intelligence approaching that of man's is *"twaddle."*

Assigning such a derogatory word to anyone who opposes one's argument is an obvious **intimidation** intent signal. Limbaugh tells us that if we agree with the *New York Times Science Report,* we are guilty of believing "twaddle," which means we are dumb enough to believe something that is "silly, weak or pretentious." Besides giving us a red flag, this is an unfortunate characterization to assign to the many devoted and intelligent researchers whose studies of dolphin behavior reflect the same conclusions reported in the *New York Times.*

5. High Protein Cows

"Take the poor cow. The May 1992 edition of Countryside Magazine has a story called, "The Last Roundup for Beef?" In it, liberal eco-pest, Jeremy Rifkin, argues that without cattle, the world would be green, well fed and peaceful. He claims that 1.28 billion cattle are now taking up 24 percent of the world's land mass, a ridiculous figure that few of the media will even challenge. Rifkin is bent out of shape because he says the cattle consume enough grain to feed hundreds of millions of people."

"The reason the cattle are eating the grain is so they can be fattened and slaughtered, after which they will feed people, who need a high protein diet. I suppose Rifkin somehow supports curbing the cow population to limit the damage they are inflicting on mankind."

Red Flags:
18, 22

The interesting thing about this presentation is that it does not contain the usual persuasive words, nor any serious intention fault. It is also relatively free of logical fallacies. The two flags that are raised, however, are waving vigorously. The first is a **personal attack** on Jeremy Rifkin. Beginning an argument by calling the author of its opposing postulate an "eco-pest" is the first sign of a weak contention. If name calling isn't enough, Limbaugh also calls Rifkin's statistics "ridiculous." Rather than explaining why the environmentalist's claims may be erroneous, he buries the subject by crying that "few of the media will even challenge" the statistics. Such a strong charge should be backed up with an explanation.

Name calling usually accomplishes the objective of **ignoring the issue** that is central to a debate. This is exactly what it does here. Rifkin's well researched conclusions, also presented in John Robbin's highly acclaimed and thoroughly documented book (Robbins, 1989), are at least worthy of discussion if one is to take issue with them. Limbaugh merely berates Rifkin's ideas with name calling, then concludes with a statement of his own he believes will prove the absurdity of Rifkin's position once and for all. He says we need all the cattle *"so we can feed people who need a high protein diet."* Predictably, this does not stand up to the facts. Nutritional science has determined that the human need for a high protein diet is not high. This is not new information. Since 1969, most studies have concluded that the average American consumes three times the total amount of protein he needs. Current recommendations are for a decrease in national protein intake, as some evidence suggests kidney function is improved if protein intake is not too high. (Vickery, 1989, p.14) In 1980, the National Research Council even reduced its recommended daily allowance from the 1968 recommendation by nearly twenty percent.

This information about "high protein" is not a digression into taking one side or the other regarding the difference of opinion between Limbaugh and Rifkin regarding potential ecological damage by cattle on the planet. It merely demonstrates how likely it is that a speaker will lead us to a false conclusion when name calling is used as a persuasive tool in his argument.

6. A Foolish Notion

"I don't understand how the same people who say we are powerful enough to destroy the earth, just by acting according to our nature, also say we are no better and no more worthy of respect than a frog. This is the great paradox of the environmentalist."

"The animal rights crowd, which is largely sympathetic toward much of the environmental fringe movement, believes there is a continuum from a mosquito to a rat to a boy. They seem to think that all life-forms on the planet, other than human beings, peacefully coexist. But humans destroy, they say. That is such a foolish notion, not only because most animals and insects depend for their very existence on consuming each other, but because humans are the only creatures

capable of cleaning up the messes made by themselves and all other creatures." (Limbaugh, 1992, p.154)

Red Flags:
7, 11, 21, 8, 24, 18, 25, 17

The first part of this argument warns of a **generalization** fallacy, as would any statement that labels an entire group as "part of a great paradox." The paradox comes from Limbaugh's apparent belief that something powerful is also superior, and is thus more worthy than anything less powerful. He does not understand how something "powerful enough to destroy the earth" could be related to a mere frog. This recurring theme of **supremacy** in Limbaugh's rhetoric continues to haunt his language. Worthy means having value or usefulness. This is more likely what environmentalists mean if they use the word to describe wildlife. Some may refer to the utility an animal has in medical research. Others see their value as a balancing factor in our delicate ecological system. Many assume their value is independent of benefit to humans. A paragraph earlier, Limbaugh may contradict himself when he says humans "are as much a part of (the world) as any of its other inhabitants . . . "(p.154) The truer paradox here is the idea that someone who "by nature" destroys its environment is more deserving of respect than one that does not. We could, perhaps, also take issue with Limbaugh's inference that man's destructiveness is an *unavoidable* result of his "acting according to (his) nature."

In both the first and second paragraphs, Limbaugh uses **emotional words** to support the anti-Darwin assumptions that underlie the argument. Most people would prefer not to align themselves with such life forms as frogs, mosquitos or rats. If these images are not enough to motivate us to choose sides, Limbaugh uses **intimidation** language. If we believe humans destroy their environment and animals do not, we are guilty of being "foolish." It is *"such a foolish notion, not only because animals and insects depend for their very existence on consuming each other, but because humans are the only creatures capable of cleaning up the messes made by themselves and all other creatures."*

This rationale uses a faulty **generalization**. Not all animals and insects consume each other. Many are vegetarians. Humans also consume other animals. As for the idea that only humans can clean up "the messes made by themselves and other creatures," the word "only" red flags the possibility of both an **absolute** fallacy and a **supremist** intent. It brings us to the questions, "Is it true that no other creatures, such as ants, bees, buzzards or even maggots, clean up its mess or the mess of others?" and "What does this have to do with the point of the argument?"

Limbaugh also uses **pacing** to sell us a **false cause** fallacy. The pacing is accomplished with the conjunctive phrase, "but because humans are the only creatures . . ." By so doing, he leads us to believe it is foolish to think that humans destroy *"Because animals eat each other"* or *"because humans are the only ones who can clean up messes."*

7. Head First

Since this argument is long, I will do my best to paraphrase here rather than state it verbatim. It begins with a Limbaugh **anecdote.**

"I once asked a long-haired maggot-infested FM-type environmentalist wacko who he thought was threatening the owl." (Limbaugh, 1992, p. 161)

The "wacko" supposedly answers that man is the enemy. Limbaugh then asked him if he would say *"that the human species is far superior to any other species?"* The wacko won't say. Limbaugh says to the reader. *"You see, they don't want to admit that, but it's true."*

He continues, *"Then I closed in for the conversational kill."* he asks the wacko, *"Would you say the owl has evolved to a superior position over the mouse?"* The wacko agrees. Limbaugh then describes what happens when *"animals eat each other"* in detail. *"The mouse gets eaten by an owl head first, with its little legs dangling out."* He says, *"That's how nature really is; these animals don't even cook their own food out there. At least we do that."*

The Bum's Rush

"So I have the environmentalist in a corner. So, is it not the responsibility of the mouse to adapt to the potential threat of the owl? ... Well, there you have it ... If the owl can't adapt to the superiority of humans, screw it."

"Now, I know that sounded heartless. But my argument follows simple, pure logic. If a spotted owl can't adapt, does the earth really need that particular species so much that hardship to human beings is worth enduring in the process of saving it?" (Limbaugh, 1992, p. 162)

Red Flags:
1, 6, 7, 9, 22

The essential fallacy in this argument is **ignoring the issue**. Limbaugh believes he has his manifestation of an environmentalist "in a corner." The "maggot-infested wacko" supposedly accepts Limbaugh's **metaphor**. The analogy, however, does not work. **Superiority** the owl has over the mouse relates only to a food chain relationship between a single prey and a single bird of prey. The environment issue, however, relates the "superiority" of man to the extinction of an entire subspecies. Even the owl in the story is wise enough to know the difference between a meal and extermination. The owl realizes mice must remain healthy and abundant for the owl's sake. Like most animals, it kills only what it needs for survival.

To sway the listener, Limbaugh depends, paradoxically, on Darwin. Although he begins by making it appear he is just beating his opponent at his own game, it is the 'simple, pure logic' of survival of the fittest that ultimately wins his point. *"If a spotted owl can't adapt, does the earth really need that particular species so much that hardship to human beings is worth enduring the process of saving it."*

This reliance on Darwin contradicts his usual fundamentalist position that defines man's **supremist** relationship with animals. In this argument, however, he uses survival of the fittest to defend man's right to dominate the spotted owl into extinction. Limbaugh hides his strategy of "using whatever works" with **humor** and **questions.** His joke about animals not cooking their food follows the **emotional words** describing a little mouse being eaten by the owl, "head first, with its little legs dangling out." He then gives humans another leg up with his tag statement, *"At least we (cook our food)."* This tag is weak, however, since it **generalizes** that humans never eat raw foods.

The questions, *"Does the earth really need . . .?"* and *"Do you hear anyone making the case . . . ?"* allow for him to insert the answers he wants us to believe. One of his answers implies that, since thousands of species have become extinct, we should not worry about another. As we have already learned, this is a **false cause** argument. Although it is true many species became extinct without man's help, the rate of extinction since man's relatively recent impact on the earth is a more significant issue.

Limbaugh concludes his presentation with, *"That's the wrong set of priorities, my friends."* What he is referring to is the choice between the jobs that would be lost to save the spotted owls. There is no fallacy or serious persuasion effort in this conclusion. Perhaps the choice in favor of the spotted owl and its habitat is the wrong priority in this case. Perhaps not. If it is the wrong priority, Limbaugh's arguments did not effectively bring us to such a conclusion. Furthermore, such generalizations contribute to preventing people from contemplating such choices on a case by case basis.

Doing the Limbaugh

> *Omens were as nothing to him and he was*
> *unable to discover the message of prophecy till*
> *the fulfillment had brought it to his very door.*
> --Joseph Conrad in *Typhoon*

8. Dr. Waters

"My first guest is an editorial from the Wall Street Journal. My second guest today, who also agrees with our first guest, is a position paper from Science and Environmental Policies Public Project from Washington, D.C." (Limbaugh laughs loudly for about 42 seconds here) *"I want you to remember you've heard this all before. You've heard most of this in philosophical form and theoretical form FROM MY MOUTH* (emphasis his)."

At this point Limbaugh reads and paraphrases from the Wall Street Journal editorial.

"Dr. Joe Waters, at Cal Tech, a top scientist with NASA's Ozone research project, warns that in his view there will not be a large ozone hole this year." (Limbaugh reads "this year" softly.)
"As NASA has been the first to acknowledge, their

106

own report is not finished. The Journal editorial goes on to say that environmental science has become an area fraught with political pressure. It is simply not clear to us that real science drives policy in the ozone area."

"NASA's Michael Kurylo himself noted that a recent "Time Magazine" cover story on the subject played on sensationalism and said that scientists have mixed feelings about press releases."

"That's from our first guest. And it can be summarized by saying that there is NO OZONE DEPLETION (Emphasis his.) *No hole has been found."*

Limbaugh then reads from the second article:

"Principal project scientist, James Anderson, in "Science News," of February 8th of this year, could only vaguely predict the development of a hole during some year in the near future. (Limbaugh reads,"near future," quickly.) *Perhaps in the decade to come."* Then Limbaugh says:

"Make no mistake about it folks. Even those who want you to believe that there is an ozone hole haven't got the courage to lie about it. They are attempting to convince you that there might be, and the fact that there might be is reason enough to begin drastic measures that will have great economic harm and impact in order to fix them." (Limbaugh, Radio Broadcast, August 4, 1991)

Red Flags:
6, 11, 26, 7, 13, 21, 20

Absolute phrases like, "Make no mistake" usually point to the absolute certainty intent fallacy. An open-minded investigation of facts is not always behind such an intent. The absolute tone of voice is another clue. Limbaugh's laughing segment is another red flag. The **humor** is not only designed to relax the listener and bring him into rapport with Limbaugh, it also sets the stage for his argument that it is ridiculous to believe there is ozone depletion. **Emotional words** like, "drastic" and "great" add to this mood.

Two fallacies that are obvious in the above statement are **burden of proof** and **misrepresentation of reference.** In the first one, Limbaugh infers, based on his interpretation of the articles, that no one has proved there is ozone depletion. Therefore, his contention that there is no such thing stands until someone proves there is.

The **misrepresentation of reference** signal is the most blatant fallacy, however. After listening to the above radio broadcast, I personally called Dr. Joe Waters at Cal Tech's Top Secret Jet Propulsion Laboratories to get a "from the horse's mouth" clarification of the Wall Street quote (Something you would expect a broadcast journalist to do before making such emphatic claims?) After introducing myself, and telling him what Limbaugh read on the air, here is what Dr. Waters told me on the phone. I quote directly:

"Our scientific work is often misrepresented by extremists on both sides. My statement about the ozone hole not getting any bigger THIS WINTER (emphasis his) was based on a variety of environmental factors that appear to be slow-

ing down ozone depletion temporarily."

I then asked if this meant ozone depletion was not a problem. He replied;

"No, this is not a reason for any less concern. In fact, there are reasons for extreme concern for the human population."

Remember, Joe Waters was the main reference Limbaugh used to come to the conclusion that there is no ozone problem! In the following sentence, Limbaugh closes with a **generalization** fallacy.

"That's from our first guest and it can be summarized by saying that there is no ozone depletion."

The only thing Limbaugh quoted Michael Kurylo as saying was that "scientists have mixed emotions about press releases." How does it follow that this means there is no ozone depletion? If Limbaugh was unsure of Kurylo's stand on the ozone issue, he could have read the edition of a conservative magazine he often quotes. On April 6, 1992 *"Insight,"* featured a story on the ozone issue that agrees with Limbaugh that the ozone scare is all hype. In it both James Anderson and Michael Kurylo were quoted as having feelings quite different than those stated above. The men were interviewed at a February 3 news conference:

"We believe now that the probability of significant ozone loss taking place in any given year is higher than we believed before. 'We're not concerned with just remote regions now,' added NASA's Michael Kurylo, program manager of the Arctic expedi-

tion. 'What we're dealing with extends to very populated regions.' "
(Morrison, 1992, p. 6)

"Make no mistake about it folks, even the people who want you to believe there is an ozone hole don't have the courage to lie about it."

Here we have an ambiguous (same as **missing word**) signal. "Make no mistake about what? What kind of mistake? How does it relate to people without courage to lie? The ambiguity of the directive causes us to search for the obvious intent of the speaker. However, since we do not want to make a mistake, we might just let it pass.

As for the second half of the sentence, an **either-or** fallacy waves another red flag for us. Limbaugh's inference that "the people" (us vs. them?) need courage to lie (as opposed to the more common idea that it takes courage to tell the truth) is confusing. How have such people been getting us to believe that there is an ozone hole? They are either telling the truth (because they do not have the courage to lie) or they are telling a lie (which they cannot because they do not have the courage). My deduction would be that they are telling the truth to the best of their ability. As for their uncertainty about exactly how bad it is or what it will be like in the next decade, it seems they are being honest about this. What is happening in Limbaugh's attempt to make his argument stick is thus **either-or** logic. Either there is a provable "end of the world" ozone problem that will require using up all of our resources to fix, or there is no ozone depletion at all and we should forget entirely about the subject.

9. Pinatubo

"Mount Pinatubo in the Philippines spewed forth more than a thousand times the amount of ozone-depleting chemicals in one eruption that all the flourocarbons manufactured by wicked, diabiolical and insensitive corporations in history. So much so that respected scientists now say that a four to six percent ozone loss could--could, but may not- occur over the Northern Hemsiphere in the next two or three years. Now, wait, before you think I have just destroyed my own argument, remember this: volcanoes have been doing this for four billion years. And guess what? We still have a healthy ozone layer! Hmmm. You still don't get it? Read it again, folks. One eruption, in four billion years of eruptions- a thousand times as destructive as all man-made CFCs . . . Mankind can't possibly equal the output of even one eruption from Pinatubo, much less four billion year's worth of them, so how can we destroy ozone? In other words, Mother Nature has been attacking her own ozone for millions of years and yet the ozone is still there, and in sufficient quantities to protect Democrats and environmental wackos alike from skin cancer." (Limbaugh, 1992 p. 156)

Red Flags:
16, 7, 8, 9, 10, 28, 4, 11, 18

This version of the well known Mount Pinatubo argument is full of red flags. We will look briefly at each, begin-

ning with #16, the **face value** fallacy. When someone
who is not an expert in the field gives out this kind of
information without references, we should be concerned with the possibility of a **misrepresentation** of
the references the speaker may have used to support
his position. The ozone issue is controversial. Scientists on both sides of it admit uncertainty. How can
Limbaugh then be so absolutely certain? For example,
Limbaugh says, Mount Pinatubo spewed forth more
ozone-depleting chemicals in one eruption than all the
CFCs manufactured by humans in history. According
to Dr. James Robert Podolski, a ranking Atmospheric
Scientists with the Space Science Division of NASA's
AIMS Research Center:

"I've seen the data, most of which is not public yet.
Our ozone problem is definitely serious. The amounts of
active chlorine that we are seeing are much higher than
existed even thirty years ago. This doesn't relate to volcanoes. Volcanoes don't produce CFCs. The only form of
chlorine they potentially can inject is hydrochloric acid of
HCL. From our instruments, we know there isn't a large
change in stratospheric chlorine due to a volcanic eruption. If there had been a large injection of HCLs from a
volcano, you would expect to see more HCLs in the column measurement than would be predicted just from the
breakdown of CFCs." (KQED, 6-13-92)

Limbaugh uses emotional words to imply that criti-
cisms against manufacturers of CFCs are ridiculous

when he says, *"than all the flourocarbons manufactured by wicked, diabolical and insensitive corporations in history."* He persuades us further with the **questions,** *"Isn't it wonderful? Aren't you thrilled?"* He then tries to intimidate with the question, *"You still don't get it?"* which he answers with repetition, one of the pacing devices. *"Read it again, folks."* After repeating his message, he repeats it once again using the **missing word** technique of using a "ly" word to form another absolute, "mankind can't possibly."

Repeating his conclusion one final time, using the phrase, "in other words," to answer still another question; *"so how can we destroy ozone?"*, he resorts to a **personal attack** on environmentalists and Democrats with his usual reference to the word, "wacko." Simultaneously, he makes an absolute statement regarding skin cancer. The argument also insinuates that there is not possibly a connection between ozone depletion and the rising rates of skin cancer. This is another conclusion we would be wise to investigate further before going to the beach without our sun screen.

10. Punishment

"Now, I want to make it clear that when there is damage to the environment, there is no one who wants to fix

*it more than I do. However, I refuse to believe it is neces-
sary to attack the American way of life or to punish American people for simply being themselves. We don't have
to punish progress in order to fix the environment."*
(Limbaugh, 1992, p. 157)

Red Flags:
7, 3, 4, 10, 11, 27

Words such as "now," "again" and "here" are **emotional words** that seize our attention and focus our interest on what follows them. A professional salesperson uses
the word "now"often throughout his presentation to a
prospect. It is also used in a hypnosis session to induce
trance. "Now, you are beginning to feel more relaxed."
Since we are viewing such words as red flags, putting us
on guard for possible fallacies, knowing this function of the
word will keep us alert. Instead of giving all our attention to
what follows "now," we can focus some attention or whether
the words that follow it are valid.

The first sentence in the quoted paragraph is an obvious
rapport strategy. If we believe no one wants to fix the environment more than Limbaugh, we will be less critical of
what he has to say about the environment. He builds a **contingency**, however, into his statement. No one wants to fix
damage to the environment more than Limbaugh IF fixing
the problems does not get in the way of either progress or
lifestyle. He gives us this contingency, using such absolutes
and **missing words** as "refuse," "don't" and "simply."

The **emotional word,** "punish," warns us of the **righteous indignity** intent that lurks behind the conclusion. Limbaugh intimates that fixing the environment with legislation which mandates certain restrictions on industry is "punishment" for "progress." The many red flags required to bring us to this conclusion show how many persuasive strategies a speaker must use to get "folks" to believe such a idea. This warns us of the possibility the swan song may not be true.

11. The Cuyahoga River

"Take the Cuyahoga River, which caught fire about twenty years ago because it was filled with so much junk and sludge. We set out to clean it up. We rolled up our sleeves, and we did it. I'm sure some regulation was used, but the major factor was good old American know-how. If you go to Cleveland today, you'll see non-polluting businesses operating all along the river. The key to cleaning up our environment is unfettered free enterprise, our system of reward." (Limbaugh, 1992, p.157)

Red Flags:
16

Only one red flag warns us to research this argument's conclusion before accepting it. The pronoun, "we" is a clue that a **face value** fallacy may exist. Did Limbaugh personally participate? Does he mean all Americans rolled up their sleeves, including the environmental wackos? Since we know he disassociates with environmentalists, activists and government control of industry, we must assume that 'we" refers exclusively to industrialists. He suggests the Cuyahoga River is no longer polluted because it was cleaned up by "unfettered free enterprise." The **face value** red flag recommends we do some research on the history and status of the river. Here is a preview:

The Cuyahoga River has improved since the famous fire on it in 1969. The "major" reason for the improvement was, however, the Clean Water Act of 1972. The terrible pollution in the Cuyahoga and the Potomac Rivers were the most notable examples Senator Ed Muskie of Maine used in his battle to overcome President Nixon's veto of the clean water legislation. "Unfettered free enterprise" representatives, who worried about economic "threats to the quality of life," were behind Mr. Nixon's veto. (CRS, 1972) Senator Muskie followed the lead of many citizen and environmental groups that fought vigorously to obtain a law which ultimately would result in "fishable and swimmable" waters, with zero chemical and sewage discharge into them. (Adler, 1993)

As for the status of the river, there are still more than one hundred outflows that send a combination of sewage and storm water runoff into the river. Its lower stretch, dredged to provide a ship channel to allow the barges to carry iron ore to the steel mills is considered a "dead zone." The locals call this dead because there is virtually no oxygen left in the water in the slow flowing section of the river. The joke in Cleveland is about fish holding their breath when they swim through the area.

It seems, in Limbaugh's argument, he may have reached for the wrong key when he concludes, "*The key to cleaning up our environment is unfettered free enterprise, our system of reward.*" Apparently cleaning up the Cuyahoga River, *his* example, called for environmental activism and government regulation in addition to industrial cooperation and "know-how."

12. The Best

"*When you compare the environmental situation in America with that of other countries, we win hands down. We have the cleanest country in the world. The world has never seen anything like the United States of America. In higher education, economics, lifestyle, prosperity, form of government, and personal freedom, we are blessed with more and better than any other country. Yet, the environmental wackos go out of their way to find fault with everything in America. They criticize our profit motive, even though it's given us the most sophisticated pollution control technology in the world."* (Limbaugh, p. 158)

Red Flags:
17, 18, 16, 11

If we say "the dance caused the rain," we have a **false cause** fallacy. When Limbaugh says people should never criticize the profit motive because we have the most sophisticated pollution control, he presents a false cause fallacy. One idea does not necessarily follow the other. It was constructive criticism from environmental groups that caused the profit motive's previous disregard for pollution control to development the pollution control technology. Furthermore, having the most sophisticated technology does not necessarily include the motivation to use it. For example, New York City ranks 14th out of 37 cities in the world in sulphur dioxide pollution. Los Angeles ranks in the top ten. (The closer to number one, the worse the pollution.) (Kurian, 1991, p. 280) We may have the technology to correct this problem, but the profit motive does not yet encourage its application.

Name calling, or **personal attack**, shows up again in *"Yet, the environmental wackos go out of their way to find fault with everything in America."* This remains a warning to double check the veracity of a statement. A recent *New York Times* news service article quoted Jacques Cousteau as saying, "We are prisoners of a system that uses more resources per capita every year . . .

I'm sick and tired of seeing an oil spill every week ... " Cousteau complained of the hypocrisy and cruelty of the free market system and warned people about the self-destructive course we are on. (*Idaho Statesman,* 1-30-94) According to Limbaugh's view, Cousteau's remarks would put him at the top of the list of "wackos." Most public opinion polls would disagree.

Red flags also show **absolute** persuasion with the words, "best" and "hands down." Americans should be proud of their country for many reasons. One is that they have the opportunity to keep improving it and to learn from mistakes. When someone gives us false information, cloaked in unquestioning nationalism, before we know it we may have less to be proud of. Limbaugh says we are "more and better" than any other country in six categories. Let us not take his words at **face value** and see if he is correct. The following facts are from Kurian's 1991 edition of The **New Book of World Rankings**, from Facts on File, and Wolf's 1992 edition of **Where We Stand.** Both of these are highly reputable and thoroughly researched reference texts.

Limbaugh says we are number one in each of the following categories:

Education:
The U.S. ranks 41 out of 164 countries in male literacy rates. (Kurian, 1991, p. 242) The U.S. has the highest number of uneducated citizens of the indus-

trialized countries and is 7th in overall spending for education. (Wolf, 1992, p. 40, 53)

Economics:
Using the earning power of each nation's citizens, defined by the gross domestic product per person, the U.S. ranks 9th out of the top 21 nations. It is thus a myth that our standard of living is the highest in the world. It is only average. (Wolf, p. 10)

Lifestyle:
The U. S. ranks 15th out of 170 nations in the Quality of Life Index. (Kurian, p. 230) In life expectancy, an important indicator of general quality of life, the U.S. ranks 17th out of 195 nations.

Form of Government:
Out of 16 nations that claim democracy as their form of government, the United States leads by far in the number of known political scandals. (Wolf, p. 185) Whether greed is causal to this is up to the reader to decide. According to a panel of political experts interviewed on the Bill Moyer program, most U.S. congressional candidates require money from special interest groups to even run for congress. (Moyers, Jan.,1994) Also, fewer than 50 percent of U.S. citizens vote.

Personal Freedom:
Wolf's book rates the U.S. 13th out of 22 na-

tions in personal freedom. The **New Book of World Rankings** uses the United Nation's "Human Freedom Index" for its rating of this category. This is based on an evaluation program that considers many variables, such as travel, right to assemble, speech, political opposition, press, privacy, etc. Sweden rates the highest and Turkey rates the lowest. The U.S. is 11th out of 17 countries studied. (Kurian, p. 202)

Thus, contrary to Limbaugh's statements, the United States has plenty of room for improvement in all the areas he lists. There is nothing unpatriotic about this realization. We live in a wonderful country. Hiding our heads in the sand of nationalistic hubris will not contribute to keeping it wonderful.

Hanging in Limbaugh

> *Between two evils, I always choose the one*
> *I never tried before.*
>
> --May West

13. The Biggest Threat

"*. . . its time we reidentify today's biggest threat to the American way of life. I'm convinced it's what I call the Socialist Utopian . . . their value system is at war with the Judeo Christian tradition upon which this country was founded . . . Their God is in every fiber of nature . . . He is just as much a part of the plant and animal kingdom as He is a part of the human soul; thus their pantheistic devotion to animals and the environment. Their God did not give them dominion over nature . . . positioning them at the top rung on the hierarchy of creation, as did the Judeo-Christian God.*" (Limbaugh, p. 265)

Red Flags:
11, 21, 23, 24, 25, 26

The **supremist** intent, often accompanied by absolute intent and **absolute** persuasion language seems to be behind many of Limbaugh's statements. In the previous two groups of arguments, we revealed certain **contradictions** in application and misinterpretation relating to his use of Christianity or the Bible to support his charges against environmentalists. We see them again in this **generalization** that labels anyone who shows "devotion" to saving animals or the environment as a socialist.

Without debating issues per se, there are enough red flags to give us reason to investigate similar contradictions in this argument. After all, we may be addressing the "biggest threat" to the American way of life." This time, however, I will only suggest some appropriate questions to help the reader decide if Limbaugh has misrepresented or misinterpreted any facts.

1. The same people Limbaugh says are Utopian Socialists are the ones he says are "doomsayers." Can one seek Utopia on earth and preach doom and gloom at the same time?

2. Are activists who speak out for animal rights or a cleaner environment at 'war with the Judeo-Christian tradition upon which this country was founded?"

3. Limbaugh has said elsewhere, *"We humans had nothing to do with the earth's creation . . .we are only part of it, which is not to downplay our significance in this world. We are as much as part of it as any of its other inhabitants, both animate and inanimate."* In the argument above, he ridicules anyone who believes "God is just as much a part of the plant and animal kingdom as He is part of the human soul." Is there incongruence here?

4. Pantheisim is a doctrine that believes that nature is God, and that there is no God but the combined forces of Nature. Is this the same as believing God is a part of Nature, as Limbaugh contends?

5. Emmet Fox, a noted interpreter of the Bible, believes the Lord's Prayer is the most important teaching in Christianity. The phrase, "Thy Kingdom Come, Thy Will be done, on earth as it is in Heaven," according to Fox "means that it is our duty to be ever occupied in helping to establish the Kingdom of God on earth. That is, to say, our work is to bring more of God's ideas into concrete manifestation upon this plane. That is what we are here for." (Fox, 1979, p. 172) If this is what Christ meant when he said "On earth as it is in Heaven," would Limbaugh call Him a "socialist utopian?" If we concede that perfection on earth is impossible, but believe our efforts to strive *toward* it are valid, are we guilty of being a threat to the American way of life?

14. Hard Cases

"Kids kill their fellow students for jostling them in the hall. Human life has become cheapened. Abortion has played a role in this, and that's another reason we have to reduce its influence on our society." (Limbaugh, 1992, p. 55)

"According to a recent survey of 1900 women by the Allan Guttmacher Institute, only 7 percent of all abortions are motivated by 'hard cases.' Here is the breakdown: the mother's health, 3 percent; when the baby has a possible health problem , 3 percent; or when the pregnancy results from rape or incest, 1 percent. 16 percent had abortions because they were concerned about how a child would change their life. Some 21 percent said they couldn't afford the baby, 12 percent blamed a relationship problem, 11 percent felt they weren't mature enough, 8 percent of the

women said they had all the children they wanted. This is staggering." (Limbaugh, 1992, p. 52)

Red Flags:
7, 14, 8, 13

It is probable that teenage violence has increased in recent years. In a time sequence, it is probably true that the increase in juvenile crime occurred after much of the public discussion about abortion. It is an **after this, therefore because of this** fallacy, however, to say that abortions are responsible for the increase. The **emotional words** conveying the extreme idea that human life has been cheapened and kids kill each other in the hall for no reason adds impact to the fallacy. *"And that's another reason ..."* employs the **pacing** conjunctive, "and," to tie the unrelated premises together.

Reviewing the actual Allan Guttmacher Institute report reveals a **misrepresentation of reference** fallacy also. First of all, nothing in the survey, nor the article describing the survey, indicates anything about "all abortions." Second, no one associated with the Guttmacher Institute decided which situations were "hard cases" and which were not. Limbaugh has put only rape, incest and health risks to the mother or fetus into his "hard case" category. Using his own labels to define the other categories, he misuses the statistics and the conclusions of the authors of the report in several ways.

Table One of the study Limbaugh refers to, published in *Family Planning Perspectives,* (Torres, 1988) does not describe the reasons the 1900 women had abortions, as Limbaugh infers. Rather, it describes the most important of an average of four reasons the women had abortions. The study says that 63 percent of the women reported three to five reasons for choosing an abortion, and another 13 percent cited six to nine reasons. Only 7 percent cited just one reason for having an abortion. In other words, 93 percent of the women gave almost four reasons each for making the difficult decision.

Limbaugh's use of the statistics thus conveys a significantly slanted perspective on the facts. He implies that 21 percent of the women chose an abortion simply because "they couldn't afford the baby." The report actually shows that 21 percent said not being able to afford a baby was the most important reason of an average of four reasons. Table two shows that 45 percent of all the women cited this as one of the reasons for choosing to have their abortion. So, from this article we do not know how many women saw health risks as important issues besides the "most important" one. We all know that an accumulation of reasons tips the scales more than just one. It is possible that a combination of three to nine of the reasons other than rape, incest or health would qualify for a "hard case." The authors of the Guttmacher study themselves concluded that economic reasons for not carrying through with an accidental pregnancy were alone sufficient to characterize a difficult case. (Almost half the women listed this reason.)

"Having a baby and raising a family can be an expensive proposition. Many young, unmarried or poor women are not covered for the costs of even prenatal care and delivery. (Does this make it a health issue?) Maintaining an adequate standard of living increasingly requires that women work, and to do so they must have an adequate education. Both aims can be threatened by an accidental pregnancy, not just among young, unmarried women, but among older, married women as well." (Torres, 1988, p. 175)

We might have added **generalization** to the fallacy of Limbaugh's argument. The study involved only nineteen hundred of the 1.6 million women who had abortions from 1987 to 1988. Using only the most important reason the women in the study had an abortion, assuming this represented all 1.6 million reasons, 97,600 people chose abortions because or rape, incest or health risks. Now the "only 7 percent" figure does not seem so "staggering," as Limbaugh presumably meant it. (Probably the number would even be higher, since the nineteen hundred respondents were more likely than all abortion patients nationwide to reside in the North Central Region of the U.S., where rape and incest might not be as prevalent.)

We included an argument on abortion in our focus on environmental backlash rhetoric because of its association with overpopulation, which is an environmentalist issue. One chapter from Limbaugh's book notes this in its title, "Abortion and the Rain Forest."

15. A Moral Imperative

"I can understand some people's perplexity over the issue (of abortion). "But if there is doubt about something as all important as the existence of life isn't it morally imperative that we resolve that doubt on the side of life?" (Limbaugh, 1992, p. 57)

Red Flags:
4, 8, 9, 11, 23

Limbaugh begins his presentation with a **rapport** building statement, *"I can understand . . . ,"* as any good persuader should. He then uses the **pacing** conjunctive "But" to ask the **question** he next answers with an **absolute** word, "imperative." We should be on guard by now. Knowing previous statements of Limbaugh also tells us a **contradiction** exists in this brief, but powerful, example of persuasion.

Limbaugh infers he would not regard the possibility of a threat to life as sufficient motivation for action if the action might result in economic restraints on businesses. He admits "respected scientists now say that 4 percent to 6 percent ozone loss could occur over the Northern hemisphere in the next two or three years." (p.156) He concedes that environmentalists are attempting to convince us that *"the fact that there might be an ozone hole is reason enough to begin drastic measures that will have great economic harm and impact in order to fix them.*" If, however, he believes the rationale he uses in statement # 15 above, why doesn't he apply it in these cases? If there is doubt, why not resolve that doubt on the side of life, rather than on the side of economic impact?

Michael Fumento associates the argument he calls "erring on the side of caution" with the environmental movement and criticizes environmentalists for using it. He says, "Actually, it is not an argument at all. Rather, it is an anti-argument. It says; instead of debating this issue, let's just assume that I'm right, because if I'm not right, no one will die, but if I am right, lives will be saved." (Fumento, 1993, p. 42)

Fumento believes erring on the side of caution is what alarmists use to win their arguments because one can't prove a negative. There is some validity in his observation. However, he makes no mention of probability in it. If evidence shows it is probable that lives may be lost, then it seems appropriate to risk erring on the side of caution. Of course, I am digressing. If Limbaugh thinks that a question of life should allow us to err on the side of caution, it seems some of his positions regarding environmental issues are inconsistent with his beliefs.

16. Almost Nothing

"There are countless other examples of such hypocrisy. Take Paul Ehrlich, the doomsayer of the population control crowd. In 1968, he wrote a book called **The Population Bomb***. Almost nothing he predicted came to pass. The book bombed, so to speak, in terms of accuracy. The point Ehrlich is making is that American free enterprise is evil . . . We've got to stop listening to people who earn their money by writing books based on misinformation, that predict our doom."* (Limbaugh, 1992, p. 160)

Red Flags:
18, 6,11

Only three red flags, but enough to make us want to verify his facts before embracing them. **The Population Bomb** predicted traffic gridlock in major cities, reduction in top soil and crop yields worldwide, increased pollution, and higher rates of starvation owing to more mouths and less food production. Current resources, such as UNICEF, the United Nations Food and Agricultural Organization, the U.S. Bureau of the Census and the 11th Annual World Watch State of the World reports, show that much of this prophecy has occurred. The following recent facts were all generally predicted by Paul Ehrlich in his book back in 1969.

- slowed growth in world food supplies
- three month doubling of rice prices since August of 1993.
- billions of acres of range land wasted
- increased water shortages worldwide
- rising seafood prices
- increased groundwater pollution
- reduction in grain production output
- reduction in use of fertilizer as evidence maximum yields may have been reached for many crops
- disappearance of top soil in many regions around the world.
- two billion increase in world population from 1968 to 1990
- an increase in number of children who starved to death

"In terms of accuracy," to use Limbaugh's phrase, perhaps we should begin listening to professional researchers and teachers like Paul Ehrlich, even if they are not entirely correct in everything they say. Such people are not predicting doom. They are trying to prevent it. If doom comes upon us, it may be because unsubstantiated backlash rhetoric tells us to ignore the preventive recommendations.

17. Dogma Food

"The environmentalist wackos have also tried to criminalize much of the food we eat in an effort to change our eating habits on the basis of very flimsy evidence. Remember when they said that oat bran would reduce cholesterol? Although that was disproved, people who were skeptical about those claims

131

at the time, such as myself, were derided for daring to question the dogma." (Limbaugh, 1992, p.163)

Red Flags:
18, 7, 9, 16

Personal attacks, ("wackos") **emotional words,** ("criminalize") and **questions,** ("remember when") help persuade us to accept Limbaugh's statements at face value.Why would environmentalists want to "criminalize" food or force people to eat oat bran? The red flags tell us to ask such a question. Considering more than 50 percent of the annual fatalities in this country are due to heart attacks, most of which result from atherosclerosis, statements relating to cholesterol warrant further research.

Limbaugh is right about there being much brouhaha about oat bran and cholesterol. It was mostly advertising hype that had us believing oat bran was a major cholesterol remedy, however, not environmentalists. The cereal and bread companies, motivated by the profit motive, launched this campaign. The evidence, though, that oat bran reduces cholesterol was not and is not "flimsy." It just wasn't comprehensive. Oat bran does lower cholesterol. It is not concentrated enough to be as significant as the media suggested. Oat fiber, which is extracted from oat bran, is more effective. Also, there are other kinds of fibers that work better than either of these to help lower cholesterol.

There are many other variables about cholesterol that should be understood, but one of them is not that we should ignore the importance of fiber in our diet. Voluminous medical literature validates the fact that dangerous cholesterol levels can be lowered with certain kinds of fiber. For a thorough bibliography, see **New Facts About Fiber.** (Kamen, 1991) If environmentalists were responsible for bringing attention to the hazards of fatty foods, perhaps we should not hold it against them.

Fools Rush In

*God offers to every mind its choice between
truth and repose. Take which you please; you
can never have both.*
                                        --Ralph Waldo Emerson

18. Little Expertise

"Carl Sagen is a very gifted astrophysicist, but he comments on things about which he has very little expertise, such as global warming and nuclear winter." (1992, p. 164)

Red Flags:
8

A brief statement like this one could easily pass by us, even with our knowledge of persuasion. Then, we might pay less attention to anything Dr. Sagen ever said. The only subtle warning is the **pacing** conjunctive, "but," which connects the compliment Limbaugh gives to Sagen with his conclusion that we shouldn't pay attention to what he says about global climate. Since many dangerous fallacies begin with a true statement or a compliment, this red flag should prompt us to check the statement out.

Our inquiry relates only to whether an astrophysicist is out of his field when he talks about global warming. According to the **Encyclopedia Americana**, astrophysics "covers a vast scope, since everything that lies beyond the dominant influence of the earth falls into its domain." (Vol.2, 1993, p. 589) We may, therefore, consider Carl Sagen to be an authority on subjects relating to global climate.

19. Their Position is Absurd

"We keep hearing that trees are being chopped down and that we have fewer trees than ever before. But look at the numbers. We have more trees in this country today than when the Declaration of Independence was written. The wacko will tell you that's impossible."

"Groups like Earth First say that a fire caused by lightening is natural, so we should let it burn. It is only man made fires that are evil . . . Their position is absurd. Trees are a valuable commodity, and companies have an incentive not to overcut them if they have clear ownership rights to them." (Limbaugh, 1992, p. 186)

Red Flags:
8, 7, 18, 13

Limbaugh's objective here is to refute the claims "we keep hearing" regarding the need to preserve and replant forest areas. He uses **pacing**, again with this favorite pacing word "but" and an attention getting **emotional** word "look," to sway us to his way of thinking. Specifically, he tells us

we have more trees in this country than when the Declaration of Independence" was written. He makes sure no
one will disagree with him by implying only "wackos"
would say this is not correct. He continues with his **personal attack** strategy in his premises in the second paragraph. Here he says it is "absurd" to think that man-made
fires are more destructive than natural ones.

The red flags warrant further research. Since no references were given to support his contention, we should
find out if there has been any **misrepresentation**. Furthermore, it is important to note if his statements about
the increase in U.S. trees accurately addresses the environmentalists' call for proper forest management around
the world. If it does not, even if there are more trees in
the U.S., he is ignoring the true issue. Global deforesta-
tion, as it affects soil erosion, crops, atmosphere, animal
life and other variables that influence all countries, may
have more to do with environmentalism concerns than
just the number of trees in the United States.

The following information may shed some light on
Limbaugh's dim perspective. According to the **World
Almanac** and **U.S. Statistical Abstracts**, forests in the
U.S. covered about 850,000,000 acres in the late seven-
teen hundreds. In 1911, they covered 550,000,000 acres.
By 1992, forests covered 730,000,000. This improvement
over the past eighty years probably relates to environmental and national park legislation, as well as to private
and public reforestation programs. So, as pertains to the
United States trees, Limbaugh is only off one hundred
million acres or so, based on these statistics.

Globally, the picture is not as pretty. The **World Book Encyclopedia** says forest land once covered 60 percent of the earth's land area. Now it covers less than 30 percent. (1988, p. 390) The 1993 edition of **Encyclopedia Americana** says, "While most of the earth's land surfaces were once forested, today less than one third of its surface is covered with forests because of man's actions." (1993, p. 582)

As for Limbaugh's assertion that man-caused fire is not more "evil" than lightening fires, the **Encyclopedia of American Forests and Conservation History** tells us differently. It explains that man generally causes the most devastating fires. Slash and burn agricultural fires, logging fires and site development fires burned more acreage than all wildfires. (Davis, 1983, p. 171-174) Other fires, like the 1994 blaze in Australia, which burned more than 1.2 million acres, are often set by arsonists or by human accidents.

The reasons these fires are generally ecologically worse than lightening fires have to do with the typical frequency, intensity and duration of natural fires. For example, there is an inverse relationship between size and frequency of natural fires. Eco-systems adapt to such fires, and determine the shape of future fires. This does not often happen with man-made ones. They usually occur during conditions that would otherwise not lend themselves to a natural fire.

20. Hogwash

"Every day we are told how evil (pesticides) are-- how we've got to reduce our reliance on them. Hog-

wash! Pesticides and chemical fertilizers have pro-
vided us with an unprecedented abundance of safer
food than ever before. And, according to a recent re-
port in Investor's Business Daily, the anti-pesticide ,
pro-organic campaign may actually be hazardous to
the health of the nation. "

"That's why it is laughable that the anti-pesticide,
pro-organic lobby claims to be interested in improv-
ing America's health. Don't believe this baloney! Lis-
ten to the scientists- the experts in their fields- not the
crackpots who preach doom and gloom in furtherance
of some far-out political agenda. " (Limbaugh, 1993,
p. 177)

Red Flags:
7, 24, 5, 18, 15, 11

No one wants to be thought of as "evil." This is why
Limbaugh uses the word so often to describe how environmentalists think of you and me. We are more likely to take
sides against someone who says our behavior is evil. Then,
add the **personal attack** words used to label the people who
call us evil and we become even more ready to join in with
Limbaugh's position. In this short paragraph, Limbaugh uses
five attacking words to create his **Us vs. Them** strategy.
(Count them.) Such red flags question his conclusion that
pro-organic, anti-pesticide advocates are crackpots with no
concern for our health.

Notice Limbaugh also **paces** us with the conjunctive
word, "and" toward accepting the "Investor Business
Daily" as proof of his wisdom. This is interesting in light

of his appeal for us to listen only to "scientists (who are) experts in their fields." The **authority** he refers to is not exactly known for being a scientific resource for agricultural methods. It might also be a little biased, considering agro-chemical sales amount to almost eight billion dollars in U.S. markets alone. (*Chemical Marketing Reporter*, May 31, 1993, p.5) Such a big business would resist anti-pesticide proponents.

The pesticide issue is a controversial one. Some experts believe pesticides make food unsafe. Others say the hazard is not very significant compared with other EPA concerns. Experts on both sides of this part of the pesticide debate, however, agree about its danger to agricultural workers, who suffer more fatalities per capita than mining or construction owing to inhalation of pesticide dust. (Blake, 1993, p. 76) Many are also concerned with serious groundwater contamination from the run off of pesticides. A minimum of twenty carcinogenic chemicals have been found in groundwater in at least twenty-four states. (EPA, 1987) The Environmental Protection Agency also estimates many animal species are jeopardized by pesticide use.

In spite of the possible hazards of pesticides, Limbaugh is correct when he says a sudden withdrawal of pesticide use would hurt the economy and reduce our supply of food. We do currently depend on pesticides to protect crops. A change to organic agriculture would have to be gradual. This would require much planning, and we would need more applied research relating to large scale organic technologies. The economics of organic farming have not been sufficiently studied to know how viable this aspect of the equation would be. There is some evidence that the change would be beneficial, however. Land would remain productive longer, and there would be less soil erosion. (**Encyclopedia Americana**, 1993, Vol. 21) We would not have to worry about possible hazards on our food and in our water. Agricultural workers would have a safer working environment. In any case, the idea that pro-organic, anti-pesticide supporters are laughable crackpots who are not interested in the health of people is now exposed as an invalid perspective.

21. Powerful Forces

" The fact is, we couldn't destroy the earth if we wanted to. (Warning, common sense is found in the next sentences. Skip them if you can't cope with it!) The earth is over four billion years old. The arch enemy of nature, man, has been on the planet no more than 200,000 years. Man cannot even come close to creating the powerful forces of nature . . . even if we dedicated all of our mental and physical resources to destroying the planet . . . we couldn't do it." (Limbaugh, 1992, p.155)

Red Flags:
8, 11, 28

The first sentence here is essentially true. Totally destroying the earth, however, is not what environmentalists mean by the phrase, "saving the planet." More likely, they are talking about saving the quality of those things they believe are a vital part of the earth experience. If rivers and oceans and forests die, and we can no longer breathe the air, the earth will most likely eventually recover. Our children, grandchildren and generations to come, would pay a terrible price, however, if any members of our species continued to exist amid such conditions. As Bertrand Russel said, "We must care about a world one will not see."

Once Limbaugh sets us up with the fact about the earth, he then warns us (**intimidates**) that if we do not believe what he says next, we have no "common sense." His argument continues with the following premises:

(**1**) The earth is over four billion years old.
(**2**) Man has been on the planet only 200,000 years.
(**3**) Therefore, man cannot come close to creating the powerful forces of nature.

There is no logic fallacy here. There is only an absence of logic. The impact we have had on the earth is especially significant *because* of our relatively short history on it. The rate of species extinction is just one example we have already mentioned. Such illogic should force us to give more thought about Limbaugh's conclusion which infers man cannot come close to creating the powerful forces of nature and therefore cannot destroy nature.

Although it is may be accurate to say that man, even with nuclear power, cannot equal the force of a volcanic eruption or a hurricane, we certain have the capability of powerful destruction.

Consider the atomic bomb, for example. On July 16, 1945, at a site called Trinity, a bomb equal to only twenty tons of TNT was tested. The explosion released energy equal to all the energy produced and consumed in the United States in half a minute. (**Encyclopedia Americana,** 1993, p. 643) A one hundred-foot steel tower the bomb was mounted on completely *vaporized* after the explosion. This was in 1945, just before Hiroshima and Nagasaki, events that took more lives than most natural disasters. Today, science and technology have advanced the destructive capability of a nuclear device. Instead of being equal to only twenty tons of TNT, the energy that can be release now is equal to one million tons of TNT! (p.643)

A million tons of TNT would be a significant force, no doubt. Whether it would come close to the power of nature, however, is a moot point, since the destruction of nature by man does not require forces of such magnitude. Widespread pollution of the oceans is not caused by power expressed in energy units. A more significant concern relating to Limbaugh's statement about man's incapability to be potentially destructive, *"even if we dedicated all of our mental and physical resource,"* may be worth considering, however. This relates to a frightening combination of his **Us vs. Them** attitude, his naivety regarding our potential for destruction, and the number of people who are persuaded by Limbaugh. Some of statements, like the one below, give credence to this concern.

"You've heard all this mumbo-jumbo: How dare we bomb people in El Salvador? What gives us the right to destroy the ozone? Why, if we would just develop an understanding with the Russian people, maybe they would realize we don't want to bomb them back to the Stone Age. (Actually, the stone age would be a giant leap forward for most Russians.)" (Limbaugh, 1992, p. 262)

22. Degree of Savagery

"In fact, while there were certainly atrocities against Indians by White people, there were just as many- and probably to a greater degree of savagery-committed by other Indians. Also, there are more American Indians alive today than there were when Columbus arrived or at any other time in history. Does that sound like a record of genocide?" (Limbaugh, 1993, p. 68)

Red Flags:
3, 8, 9, 17

In his text on persuasion, Ross says the most treacherous fallacy is one that starts with facts. (Ross, 1981, p.170) As in statement number twenty-one, Limbaugh again begins with a probably valid premise, then moves to a fallacious conclusion. Yes, "there were certainly atrocities against Indians by white people." Using a **pacing** technique, Limbaugh makes this fact contingent on his next statement, which may not be valid. He does this with the word, "While." In essence, he says, "While you believe this undeniable fact, also believe that there were just as many atrocities committed by other Indians." In other words, he tells us to believe Indians murdered other Indians more often than white people did during the short one hundred years of American history in question. This conclusion is remarkably incorrect, according to the information in texts such as those published by the National Geographic Society and the Smithsonian Institute on the American Indian. (Taylor, 1992, & Billard, 1979)

Using another **pacing** word, "also," Limbaugh brings us back immediately to a truer statement, before we have time to question his incorrect allegation. He says, *"Also, there are more American Indians alive today than there were when Columbus arrived, or at any other time in history."* He then uses a **question** to maneuver us into accepting his second and final fallacy, specifically that white man never perpetrated genocide on Native Americans.

To prove his conclusion wrong, it is not necessary to read the abundant literature documenting the U.S. policy of genocide in the early part of nineteenth century. All we need to do is use the same records Limbaugh probably used when he concluded that there are more Indians living today than *"when Columbus arrived."*

According to the **Concise Dictionary of American History,** "A minimum estimate sets native populations north of Mexico at 1.1 million in 1492." (1983, p. 490) Not-with-standing the potential errors that must have occurred when trying to count all the Indians and Eskimo back in 1492, we will assume, for Limbaugh's argument, that this is an accurate minimum estimate. According to the 1992 **Statistical Abstract of the United States,** there were 1,959,000 Indians, Eskimo and Aleuts in the same geographical area in 1990. Therefore, this premise of Limbaugh's may be correct. The Indian population, if we assume the minimum estimate of 1492 is accurate, increased by around eight hundred thousand since Columbus discovered America.

"Does this sound like a record of genocide?" It does when we compare the 1402 estimate with the U.S. census taken in 1870. According to relatively accurate U.S. records, there were only 25,734 Indians alive in the territory north of Mexico in 1870. The Indian population did not start making a comeback until after we stopped the genocide that, along with white man's disease, decimated their numbers during the previous fifty to one hun-

dred years. In fact, significant increases in Indian population did not occur until after World War One. (See **1939 Statistical Abstract**, Table 14, p. 11, Population by race in Cont. U.S. 1972-1930) An analogy to Limbaugh's argument would be "since there may be more Jews alive in Germany today than there were in 1946, there was no holocaust!"

Limbaugh may have chosen to make his Indian argument because he is upset that *environmentalist wackos* romanticize the Indian way of life. He says they do this because it is fashionable. Although there probably is some of this going on, most educated environmentalists know that Indians possess the same tragic flaws as any other humans. Their general philosophy and understanding of the balance and harmony of nature, however, does touch upon a truth that resonates in the hearts of those who honor their ideas about living with nature.

23. We Are Only Part of It

"We humans had nothing to do with the earth's creation, its placement, or its functioning. We are only part of it, which is not to downplay our role or significance in this world. We are as much a part of it as any other of its inhabitants, both animate and inanimate; as much as a redwood tree or a spotted owl, as much

a part of it as a glacier. But . . . "(Limbaugh, 1992, p. 154)

Red Flags:
NONE

Here, Limbaugh uses the strategy of leading with an undeniable premise to begin his argument about man's inability to destroy. It is a well constructed paragraph. Most people would agree with what it says. It even *resonates*. If we ignore what follows the conjuctive "but," as I have chosen to do, Limbaugh's statement might even be a contribution to the literature of environmentalism. What a positive note to end on!

CONCLUSION

No man can reveal to you aught but that which already lies half asleep in the dawning of your knowledge.

--Kahil Gibran

Gibran's advice is complete. We do, however, often behave contrary to what we know instinctively is right. Plato said, "When the mind is thinking, it is talking to itself." When we talk to ourselves, we use the language that surrounds us, even if it conflicts with our "better judgment." Backlash rhetoric takes advantage of this cultural diaogue. The more we are told environmentalism is "hype", the more likely the backlash words will become a part of our self-talk. Unless, of course, we remain critical of what we hear.

The language of our culture gives both purpose and momentum to the backlash movement. Burke said, "Motives cannot be separated from man's linguistic nature because motives are distinctly the products of the language." (Fisher, 1970, p.25) As we have seen, many such motives relate to interpretations of the Bible, especially concerning "guilt." Others come from human sciences that de-

148

pend upon the existence of a realm in which man is entirely detached from nature.

The language of money and advertising also influences our motives to act in ways that may be deleterious to the environment. Al Gore mentions this source of motivation in **The Earth in Balance.**

"We have become so seduced by industrial civilization's promise to make our lives comfortable that we allow the synthetic routines of modern life soothe us into an unauthentic world of our own making." (Gore, 1991, p. 240)

Of course, Thoreau is most famous for his eloquence on this potential threat to man's future. His words tell us that change toward a less consumptive style of life can have positive value for all of us, individually and collectively. As long as this idea is seen as a negative, however, there will continue to be a war between the environmentalists and the "backlashers."

This is not to say that commercial advertising, per se, is the cause of this war between people who disagree about who we are and how we ought to live. We do, however, let it define us more than we should. If we allow advertising to persuade us that we can and should have all pleasures at our fingertips, then we are to blame for perspectives that may ultimately cause us harm. In his book, **Recapturing the Spirit of Enterprise**, George Gilder says it another way:

"If the opinion leaders of society prescribe the unhindered pursuit of individual pleasures as the goal of life . . . capitalists will rush forward to serve this public mood and will generate the externalities it entails." (Gilder, 1992)

Admittedly, we cannot go back to what Limbaugh calls "the stone age." But neither can we continue with the unrestrained policy of individualism, which places a priority on particular wealth rather than global health. The language of "rugged individualism" that helped inspire the American dream must be expanded. Once, it produced Daniel Boone and Henry Ford. Now it produces the Marlboro Man. The former represented vision and courage. The latter represents cancer. Rather than letting one company lure us into smoking with image of the rugged cowboy, we are wiser to heed the message of the community suggesting we stop the habit.

An emphasis on cooperation instead of individuation is neither utopian nor socialistic as the *backlashers* would have us believe. Alexander Solyhenitsyn said, "the salvation of humankind lies only in making everything the concern of all." Individualism demands an appreciation for objective limits that allow for the welfare of all things, "both animate and inanimate."

The environmental debate will accomplish little good until it becomes a discussion about education, not about propaganda. Educators seek to learn and teach mutual understanding that benefits everyone concerned about an issue. Propagandists advocate causes, not necessarily for the good of all. Both may use strategies of persuasion, but we can only depend on true educators to use them ethically.

As long as there are "sides" to the environmental debate, we should not anticipate that many orators who represent one side or the other will soon change into this idealistic form of information sharing. Neither will we stop advertising's powerful tactics of persuasion, no matter how misleading they may be. We are not likely to change our verbs and nouns to make them more conducive to a 'holistic and careful attitude toward the natural environment."(Chawla, 1991, p. 253). Simplifying our lives and consuming less is also not something many of us will do voluntarily. George Santayana has recognized this probability:

"To be poor in order to be simple, to produce less in order that the product may be more choice and beautiful, and may leave us less burdened with unnecessary duties and useless possessions that is not an ideal articulate in the American mind."

What we can do, however, is influence positive change by being more careful with our language, and more attentive to the language of others. It is through language that we distort our understanding of the world. If we understand its power and remain critical of its message, we will not allow ourselves to commit the crimes against nature and humanity we have perpetrated in the past.

We can thus avoid the potential hazards of environmental backlash rhetoric if we use our understanding of pursuasive language. We might begin by taking advantage of the "bright side" of the backlash movement. Its contribution is that it may help prevent us from believing in our doom. A study of psychology shows that we tend to realize what we fear. It is thus important that we not imagine those worse-case scenarios that could result from our careless regard for the world around us. If enough of us believe something strongly enough, it may come true. If environmental backlash stops a collective belief in our demise, it will be of value.

On the other hand, positive images only manifest themselves when we are on track and if we are working hard. For example, positive thinking helps prevent illness, but not if we continue to eat poorly, take drugs, avoid exercise and live with too much stress. Furthermore, we alone are ultimately responsible for choosing which course is the best one to take. If we know their intentions and techniques, fallacious persuaders cannot influence our decisions. As long as we continually look for the "red flags" of persuasion, we will not acquiesce to fallacy. Then, no longer susceptible to "the bum's rush," we can chart a proper course for life on our planet.

References Cited

Adler, Robert W., *The Clean Water Act, 20 Years Later,* Island Press, Washington, D.C., 1993

Adorno, T.W., Frenkel-Brunswik, E., Levinson, D.J, and Sanford, R.N., *The Authoritarian Personality,* Harper, NY, 1950

Arterburn, Stephen & Felton, Jack, *Toxic Faith*, Thomas Nelson Pub., Nashville, 1991

Barnard, Neal, D.,"The Psychology of Abuse" in *The Animal's Agenda,* June, 1991

Benford, Gregory, "The Designer Plague" in *Reason,* Vol.25, No.8, Jan.,1994

Billard, Jules, ed. *The World of the American Indian,* National Geographic Society, Washington, D.C., 1979

Bittle, C.N., *The Science of Correct Thinking*, Bruce Pub., Chic.,1950

Blake, R., "Perils in the Field", *Occupational Health and Safety*, Vol.62, Issue 5, May, 1993

Bittle, C.N., *The Science of Correct Thinking*, Bruce Pub., Chic.,1950

Bloom, Allan, *Closing of the American Mind*, Simon & Shuster, NY, 1987

Brown, Lester,ed., *State of the World*, W.W. Norton, NY, 1994

Cayce, Lynn, *Earth Changes*, Edgar Cayce Foundation, 1987

Chawla, Saroj, "Linguistic and Philosophical Roots of our Environmental Crisis, in , *Environmental Ethics*, Vol. 13, Fall, 1991, p. 253

Chemical Marketing Reporter, "Agro-Chemical Sales Near Eight Billion Dollars in U.S. Markets", Vol.243, Issue,22, May 31, 1993

Concise Dictionary of American History, Charles Scribners & Sons, 1983

Congressional Research Service (CRS), *History of Water Pollution Control Act Amendments of 1972,* 93rd Cong.,137

Dietrich, Daniel, ed., "Training College Students as Critical Receivers of Public Persuasion" in *Teaching About Double Speak"* National Council of Teachers in Engish, Urbana, 1976

Ehringer, Douglas, *Influence, Belief and Argument: An Introuduction to Responsible Persuasion,* Scott, Foreman & Co., Glenview, 1974

Enclopedia Americana, Grolier, Inc. 1993

Estes, Clarissa Pinkola *The Creative Fire*, Sounds True, Boulder, 1991 (her version of wolf myth on tape)

Fisher, Jeanne, *An Analysis of Kenneth Burke's Persuasion Theory,* A Ph.D. dissertation, University of Michigan, 1970

Fox, Emmet, *The Sermon on the Mount*, Harpers, NY, 1979

Fumento, Michael, *Science Under Siege*, William Morrow Co., NY, 1993

Gaus, Andy, *The Unvarnished New Testament, A New Translation from the Original Gree*k, Thanes Press, Maine, 1991

Gildern, George, *Recapturing the Spirit of Enterprise*, ICS Press, S.F., 1992

Gordon, George N., *Persuasion: The Theory and Practice of Manipulative Communication*, Hasting house, NY, 1992

Gore, Al, *The Earth in Balance:Ecology and the Human Spirit,* Houghton-Mifflin, Boston, 1992

Herd, J. & Moite, Donald, *Modern Perusasion Strategies*, Prentice-Hall, 1984

Jacobs, Don Trent, *Executive Fitness,* MacMillan, N.Y. 1981

The Bum's Rush

The Bum's Rush

Jacobs, Don Trent, *Patient Communication for First Responders and EMS Personnel: The First Hour of Trauma,* Prentice-Hall, Englewood Cliffs, 1991

Jacobs, Don Trent, *Physical Fitness for Public Safety Employees*, NFPA, Boston, 1981

Jaynes, Julian, *The Origins of Consciousness in the Breakdown of the Bicameral Mind,* Grune &Stratton, 1964

Kamen, Betty, *New Facts About Fiber,* Nutrition Encounter, Novato, 1991

Keen, Sam, *The Passionate Life,* Harper & Row, NY, 1983

Keen, Sam, *Fire in the Belly,* Bantam, NY, 1991

Korzybski, Alfred, *Science and Sanity,* Int.Non-Aristotelian Library Pub., 1933

Kurian, George, *The New Book of World Rankings,* 3rd ed., Facts on File, NY, 1991

Lincoln Library of Essential Informatiion, "Forestry", The Frontier Press, NY, 1969

Lee, Alfred, "The Analysis of Propaganda: A Clinical Summary", in *American Journal of Sociology,* September, 1945

Limbaugh, Rush, *The Way Things Ought to Be,* Pocket Books, NY, 1992

Limbaugh, Rush, *See I Told You So,* Pocket Books, NY,1993

McClung, Robert, *Lost Wild Worlds,* William Morrow Co., 1976

McDougal, Curtis, D., *Understanding Public Opinion,* William Brown Co., NY, 1966

Moine, Donald, *Unlimited Selling Power,* Prentice-Hall, Englewood Cliffs, 1990

Morrison, Micah, "The Ozone Scare,"in *Insight,* Vol. 8, No. 14, April 6, 1992, p. 6

Moyers, Bill, *Bill Moyer's Journal,* #BMJ-5, 1-28-94

O'Rourke, P.J., *Parliament of Whores,* Atlantic Monthly Press, NY, 1991

Pope John Paul II, "Ecological Crisis: A Common Responsibility", *Message of his Holiness for the Celebration of the World Day of Peace*, Jan 1, 1990

Ray, Dixie Lee, *Trashing the Planet*, Regnery Gateway, Washington D.C., 1990

Robbins, John, *Diet for a New Amerca*, Stillpoint Publishing, NH, 1987

Roberts, Jane, *Nature of Personal Reality,* Seth Pub., Chic.,1968

Ross, Raymond, *Understanding Persuasion*, Prentice-Hall, Englewood Cliffs, 1981

Shipley, Joseph, *Dictionary of Word Origins*, Philosophical Library, NY, 1985

Spraeger, Thomas A., *The Irony of Liberal Reason*, University of Chicago Press, Chicago, 1981

Statistical Abstract of the United States, U.S. Department of Commerce, Washington, D.C., 1992

Swineburne, Richard, *Faith and Reason*, Oxford Press, Oxford, 1981

Taylor, Colin F., Ed., *The Native Americans*, Smith Mark Publishers, NY, 1992

Torres, Aida, &Forrest, Jacqueline, "Why Do women Have Abortions?" in *Family Planning Perspectives,* Vol.20, No.4, July, 1988

Toulmin, Stephen, *The Uses of Argument*, Cambridge University Press, Cambridge, 1964

Vickery, Donald & Fries, James, *Take Care of Yourself,* 3rd Ed., Addison-Wesley, Reading, 1989

Wilson, Glenn D., ed. *The Psychology of Conservatism*, Academic Press, NY, 1973

Wolf, Michael, *Where We Stand,* Bantam books, 1992

World Almanac, Press Publishing co., 1912

World Book Encyclopedia, Vol.7, 1988

Bibliography

Berry, Thomas, *The Dream of the Earth*, Sierra Club Books, S.F., 1988. A collection of essays about a more harmonious relationship between humans and the environment.

Darwin, Charles, *The Origin of Species by Means of Natural Selection*, Collier books, NY, 1962. It is worth reviewing this information, in spite of its general familiarity. I recommend complimenting it with Goodman's book, The Genesis Mystery.

Fox, Matthew, *Original Blessing*, Bear and Co., Santa Fe, 1986. This book addresses the issue of Christian guilt I have proposed may fuel environmental backlash.

Goodman, Jeffrey, *The Genesis Mystery*, Times Books, NY, 1983. The author presents a scholorly hypothesis that a spiritual factor must be added to Darwin's evolution theory in order to make sense of the unique intelligence and language of human beings.

Henderson, Hazel, *Paradigms in Progress:Life Beyond Economics*, Knowledge Systems Inc., Indianapolis, 1991. The author addresses economical factors that relate to the challenges of ecology.

Patton, Forest, *Force of Persuasion*, Prentice-Hall, Englewood Cliffs, 1986

Pratkanis, Anthony, *Age of Propaganda*, W.H.Freeman, N.H.,1992. A discussion of everyday uses and abuses of persuasion.

Swimme, Brian and Berry, Thomas, *The Universe Story*, Harper, S.F., 1992. The authors explore humanity's place in the evolving cosmos.

Wilson, Edward O. *Biophilia,* Harvard University Press, Cambridge, 1984. This is a collection of many essays explaining the importance of biodiversity.

Index

A

Abortion 11, 124-127
    See also Guttmacher Institute
absolute statements 8, **30-32**, 71-73, 83, 119, 122, 128
ad hominom 36-38
    See also personal attack
advertising 37, 132, 149
affiliations, as red flag warning 8, **76-77**
after this, therefore because of this fallacy **46**, 125
agriculture 47, 138, 139,
animal and animal rights 24, 33, 80, 81, 85 108, 117
    See also dolphins
Aristotle 2, 3, 34,
atomic bomb 142,
authority 3, 8, **19-20**, 31, 57, 75, 78, 89, 139

B

backlash ix, x, 1, 5, 6, 127, 131, 148, 150, 152
Barnard, Neil 67
Bible, The Holy 86-91, 148
Bloom, Allan 6, 72
Burden of Proof fallacy 8, **50-52**, 96, 108
Burke, Kenneth 86, 148

C

cancer 111, 113
Cal Tech 106

159

cholesterol 131-133
circular reasoning 8, **46-47**, 84, 96, 111
civilization 24, 69, 71, 149
competition, *See winning*
conjunctives, *use of in perusasion* 24-25, 101, 127, 134
conservative 36, 64, 65, 109
contingency fallacies 8, **14**, 84, 114, 119
contradiction 8, 38, **57-58**, 67, 84, 87, 119, 122, 128
Cortez, Gregorio, *The Ballad of* 56
Cousteau, Jacques 77, 118-119
Creation 86 *See also Bible*
CREDIBLE , *steps of effective persuasion* 33
Cuyahoga River 115-117

D

Darwin, Charles, *theory of evolution* 80, 84-85, 101, 103-104 , 157
dolphins 95-97
doomsayer 18, 54, 123, 130, 152
double bind 8, **12-13**, 31, 92, 125

E

economics ix, 117, 129 140, 148
education 48, 117, 119
Ehrlich, Paul 47, 54, 130
        See also **Population Bomb, The**
either-or fallacy 8, **52-53**, 92, 96, 110, 125
emergency, *medical use of persuasive language* 15, 32
emotional words 2, **21**, 31, 57, 82, 96, 101, 104, 114-115, 118, 125
enterprise *See free enterprise*
environment and environmentalists ix, 1, 4, 6, 12, 24, 38, 48, 64, 77,
        80, 85, 87, 113-114, 117, 119, 129
        See also backlash
environmentalist "wacko" 12, 26, 38, 63, 102, 113, 132, 133, 135, 146
EPA (Environmental Protection Agency) 139
extinction 103-104, 141

F

face value 8, **47-45**, 87, 115, 119, 121
fallacy 13, **34-78**, 64, 84, 112, 119
    see also fallacies by name from T.O.C.
false cause fallacy 8, **48-49** 101, 104. 118
FDA 55
"feminazi" 12, 38
fire, ecological considerations 15, 49, 115, 135-137
forests 48, 135-137
free enterprise 11-12, 48, 65, 119, 130, 150
freedom 11, 21, 48, 57, 72, 77, 117, 143

G

General Semantics 30
    See also semantics
Generalization 8, 28, 35, **53-55**, 82, 93, 100-101, 109-110, 123, 127,
genocide 11, 45, 143-145
God 3, 28, 39, 86, 88-89, 91-94, 114, 122-124 *See also Bible*
Gore, Al 46, 88, 116, 149
government 11, 55, 84, 112, 120
groundwater 42-43, 131, 137-139
guilt ix, 36, 65, 83, 85-86, 113, 118, 148, 157
Guttmacher Institute 124-126, 128

H

Heisenberg 5,
humanism 86, 88
humor 8, **20-21**, 83, 108
hypnosis 3, 26, 32, 33, 75, 78, 114, 138,
hypocricy 50, 68

I

ignoring the issue 8, **56-57**, 98, 103, 131
Indian, American 45, 143-146

information 3, 6, 67, 72, 98,131
Intimidation 8, 47, 75-76, 83, 95, 96, 101, 141

J

Jacobs 32, 41, 52
Jaynes, Julian 3
Jefferson, Thomas 34, 91

K

Keen, Sam 6, 63, 68

L

language 2, 4, 9, 21, 31, 33, 35, 36, 87, 151 *See also linguistics*
legislation 43, 67, 115, 139
Liberal 13, 28, 38, 48, 60, 64-66, 97
Limbaugh , Rush *See Table of Contents for Topic Heading*
linguistics 32, 64, 87
logic 2, 34-36, 57, 141

M

media 31, 61
metaphor 8, **10-11**, 103
misrepresention fallacy 8, **44-45**, 87, 108, 112, 114, 125, 136
missing word strategy 8, **29-30**, 83, 110, 113-114
money 5, 11, 27, 110, 120

N

nature 80, 151
        See also environment, animals
New York Times 96, 97

O

organic 138-140, 152
ozone 106-110, 111-113, 131

P

pacing strategy (and words) 8, **23**-26, 35, 101, 128, 134, 135, 138,
    144
personal attack 8, 36, 38, **49-50**, 57, 61, 67, 98, 113, 118, 123, 130,
    132, 138
persuasion 1, 2, 6, 9, 31-35, 65, 84, 119, 152
pesticide 47, 137-140, 152
philosophy 6, 50, 85
Pinatuba, Mt. 111-113
pollution 25, 42, 116, 141, 142
population 44, 73, 80, 109, 116, 130-131
Population Bomb, The 130, 153
propaganda 36, 66-67, 151
psychology 21, 38, 64, 152

Q

questions 8, 13, **26-29,** 42-44, 66, 83, 96, 111, 113, 132, 144

R

rapport 8, **14-19,** 33, 108
Ray, Dixie Lee 85
Red Flag 4, **8,** 21, 33, 57, 77, 79, 81, 87, 114, 117, 121, 132, 134,
    135, 138, 140, 143, 147
    See Red Flag List on page 8
repetition 26, 113
Rifkin, Jeremy 97, 98
righteous indignation, *as intent signal predicting possible fallacy*
    8, **73-75,** 83, 95, 115

S

Sagen, Carl 134-135
salespersons and selling 2, 9, 12, 27, 12, 68, 75, 114,

science 5, 30, 34, 96, 119, 138
semantics 30, 94
Shaw, Bernard 61, 61, 63
socialist 53, 78, 122, 123, 124, 147, 152,
sophisms (and sophistic reasoning) 36-40
statistics 44, 98, 126
stories 8, **10-12**, 74, 82
superstition 46
supremacy 8, **68-70**, 83, 94, 100, 103 *See also supremist*
supremist 101, 104, 122
survival of the fittest 82, 84-85, 109
      See also Darwin
syllogism 35, 92

T

technology 3, 25, 72, 118, 148
The Population Bomb 130
trees 14, 45, 135, 136
      See also forest
truth 3, 17, 56, 63, 89
tyranny 22, 64, 66

U

Us vs. Them 8, 30, **62**-67, 110, 138
utopia 65, 122, 124,

V

volcano 111-112

W

"wacko" *See environmental "wacko"*
Waters, Joe 106-109
winning 22, 69, 70, 119

ABOUT THE AUTHOR

Don Trent Jacobs earned his Ph.D. in health psychology while working as a firefighter and emergency medic. This combination of experiences revealed to him the power of certain kinds of communication, and inspired him to specialize in the field of

psycholinguistics. This led to Prentice-Hall's publication of his text, *Patient Communication*. As Vice President of the Northern California Society of Clinical Hypnosis, and as an Adjunct Professor at the University of California, Berkeley, he has lectured on related subjects throughout the United States and Australia. *The Bum's Rush* is Jacobs' eighth book. He is currently working on his first non-fiction novel, *The Reversal Conspiracy*.

Don Jacobs also intimately knows the environment he is trying to protect. He navigated his own sloop through North Pacific typhoons and kayaked uncharted whitewater in the remote Copper Canyon. He has ridden hundred mile races on wild horses he captured and trained himself. These and many other outdoor adventures, chronicled in such magazines as *Great Expeditions* and *Backpacker*, have given him first hand appreciation of the wonder of nature. Living with his artist wife on their ranch adjacent to the Sawtooth National Forest, Dr. Jacobs believes we will only be motivated to protect the wilderness environment if we partake of its majesty first hand.